Better Homes and Gardens

HOUSEPLANTS

The Gardener's Collection

Better Homes and Gardens® Books

Des Moines

MEREDITH® BOOKS
President, Book Group: Joseph J. Ward
Vice President and Editorial Director: Elizabeth P. Rice
Art Director: Ernest Shelton

HOUSEPLANTS
Senior Editor: Marsha Jahns
Editor: Patricia Pollock
Art Director: Michael Burns
Copy Editors: Durrae Johanek, Kay Sanders, David Walsh
Assistant Editor: Jennifer Weir
Administrative Assistant: Carla Horner
Special thanks: John Whitman

All of us at Meredith® Books are dedicated to providing you with the information and ideas you need to garden successfully. We guarantee your satisfaction with this book for as long as you own it. If you have any questions, comments, or suggestions, please write to us at:

MEREDITH® BOOKS, Garden Books
Editorial Department, RW 240
1716 Locust St.
Des Moines, IA 50309-3023

Walk into any room that you really like and look around. Chances are, growing green plants—foliage or flowering—are part of the setting. They add something indefinable, something special. This book will help you pick the plants best suited for your home and tell you how to care for them, too.

Contents

CHOOSING HOUSEPLANTS 6

CARING FOR HOUSEPLANTS 18

PROPAGATING HOUSEPLANTS 32

DIRECTORY OF HOUSEPLANTS 40

TROUBLESHOOTING GUIDE 62

INDEX 64

Choosing Houseplants

*L*iving, growing indoor plants add color, beauty, and a sense of life to our homes. Foliage houseplants, especially, offer diversity in size, form, leaf shape, and texture. Flowering plants boost our spirits with delicate, elegant blooms. Browse through this informative chapter for tips on selecting those best suited to you.

Abundant Variety

Select plants that match your decorating needs and the growing conditions in your home.

Foliage plants are the backbone of most household plant collections. In full form year-round, they provide varied shades of green, a rich variety of textures, and shapes from massive to minute. Plants can be found to match the conditions in most any spot, from a bright window to a dim bathroom.

Flowering plants add not only bright splashes of color but also exquisite scents. Some are difficult to raise indoors or are seasonal gift plants. Others are less temperamental and bloom year after year. The secret is to match the plants' needs for light and humidity with your time and home's conditions.

Though the most well-known plants fall into the categories described below, there are many others to inspire individuality.

Ferns are a class of foliage plant with 6,000 species. These thrive in indirect light and look delicate but are deceptively sturdy.

Palms also are dramatic foliage plants. They put out new growth in the winter and are well suited to summering outdoors.

Bromeliads are easy to grow and almost foolproof, usually blessed with exotic stiff leaves and bright, bold, unusual flowers.

Succulents are a huge family of plants with great diversity, unique forms, and sculpted shapes that result from stored water.

African violets now come in tiny miniature forms.

Gardener's Tip

Very small individual plants tend to dry out quickly in small pots. Try combining several miniatures in a basket to increase moisture.

Shopping Tips

Garden centers and florist shops are the best places to look for houseplants. Choose reputable stores where plants receive proper care. Some varieties may be available only by mail or from a plant society. Be sure the company has a money-back guarantee. Rare and unusual plants can be started from seeds ordered through mail-order companies.

Buyer's Checklist

■ Examine plants before buying. Foliage plants should be lush and full, have good color and firm leaves and stem, and be free of wilted or distorted leaves.

Gardener's Tip

Look for plants showing new growth. The foliage should be natural, not covered with a film of polish or wax.

■ Unless there's a good reason to buy flowers in full bloom, choose plants loaded with buds instead. This way, you can enjoy the whole show, not just the final act.

■ Look for insects and disease where branches join the stem. Plants displayed outdoors during warmer months attract insects.

■ Check the soil with your fingers. It shouldn't be too loose or too compact. Repot any with poor soil.

■ Package plants properly for the ride home. Warm the car in winter and make sure plants are wrapped. In summer, buy plants with well-moistened soil.

■ Wind may damage large plants transported in the open; wrap in heavy plastic or cloth.

■ Once home, label the new plant with date of purchase, source, plant type, and variety.

Several firecracker flowers are in this basket. They rarely grow more than 12 inches tall and do well in a south or west window.

Plants for Different Light Conditions

HIGH LIGHT

Plants in this list need high light at certain stages of development for best growth or flowering. Many also thrive in medium light. High light in winter is comparable to medium light the rest of the year.

Aloe
Amaryllis
Asparagus fern
Banana plant
Christmas cactus
Coleus
Croton
Cymbidium
Dragon tree
Fuchsia
Gardenia
Geranium
German ivy
Gloxinia
Grape ivy
Hibiscus
Hydrangea
Jade plant
Kalanchoe
Lady's-slipper
Podocarpus

Poinsettia
Snake plant
Swedish ivy
Umbrella plant
Wandering Jew
Wax begonia
Wax plant
Yucca
Zebra plant

MEDIUM LIGHT

Keep in mind that although some plants tolerate low light, it often retards bloom in flowering plants. It can affect color, shape, size, and number of leaves in foliage plants.

Achimenes
African violet
Arrowhead vine
Avocado
Azalea
Baby's-tears
Bird's-nest fern
Boston fern
Brake fern
Caladium
Camellia
Cast-iron plant
Chinese evergreen
Corn plant

Creeping Charlie
Cyclamen
Dieffenbachia
English ivy
False aralia
Fiddleleaf fig
Holly fern
Impatiens
Maidenhair fern
Ming aralia
Moth orchid
Nerve plant
Norfolk Island pine
Peperomia
Philodendron
Pleomele
Pocketbook flower
Prayer plant
Rex begonia
Rubber tree
Schefflera
Screw pine
Spathiphyllum
Spider plant
Staghorn fern
Swiss-cheese plant
Ti plant
Tuberous begonia
Weeping fig

The screw pine needs medium light; avoid full sun.

Plants for Special Purposes

Gift Houseplants

African violet
Amaryllis
Azalea
Chrysanthemum
Cyclamen
Cymbidium
Easter lily
Gloxinia
Poinsettia

Scented Houseplants

Easter lily
Gardenia
Geranium (some)
Hyacinth
Lemon tree
Paper-white narcissus

Unusual Houseplants

Banana plant
Bird-of-paradise
Ornamental pepper
Staghorn fern

Fun for Kids

Avocado (from pit)
Banana plant (with
   patience)
Spider plant
Sweet potato
Ti plant
Venus's-flytrap

Dangerous for Kids

Azalea
Caladium
Dieffenbachia
English ivy
Geranium (some)
Hyacinth
Hydrangea
Jerusalem cherry
Philodendron
Poinsettia

Climbing Plants

Arrowhead vine
English ivy
German ivy
Grape ivy
Philodendron
Sweet potato

Hanging Plants

African violet (some)
Arrowhead vine
Baby's-tears
Creeping Charlie
English ivy
Fuchsia
German ivy
Grape ivy
Philodendron
Spider plant
Staghorn fern
Swedish ivy
Sweet potato
Wandering Jew

Large or Treelike

Avocado
Banana plant
Camellia
Corn plant
Croton
Dieffenbachia
Dragon tree
False aralia
Fiddleleaf fig
Gardenia
Hibiscus

Hydrangea
Jade plant
Norfolk Island pine
Palm
Pleomele
Rubber plant
Schefflera
Screw pine
Snake plant
Swiss-cheese plant
Ti plant
Umbrella plant
Weeping fig

Cyclamen—showy gift plants clustered here in a basket—put on a dazzling display for months.

Small or Tabletop

African violet
Baby's-tears
Cast-iron plant
Coleus
Creeping Charlie
Lady's-slipper
Peperomia
Venus's-flytrap
Wax begonia

Colorful Foliage

Caladium
Coleus
Croton

Nerve plant
Prayer plant
Rex begonia

Easy-Care Plants

African violet
Aloe
Arrowhead vine
Asparagus fern
Baby's-tears
Cast-iron plant
Chinese evergreen
Coleus
Creeping Charlie
Dieffenbachia
English ivy

German ivy
Grape ivy
Jade plant
Peperomia
Philodendron
Rubber plant
Schefflera
Snake plant
Spider plant
Swedish ivy
Swiss-cheese plant
Ti plant
Wandering Jew

Tabletop Gardens

A refreshing change of pace from the one-plant–one-pot look is a lively grouping of plants in one large container.

Indoor Forest It's easy to re-create the aura of a forest in springtime. Line a basket with a 2-inch-thick layer of moistened sphagnum moss. Fill the basket with a potting mix of equal parts peat moss, soil, and perlite. Use a small trowel or tablespoon to plant ferns. For color, add pots of miniature African violets or primulas, making sure you sink the pots in the soil.

Use lukewarm water to keep the soil slightly moist, not soggy, when it begins to dry. Set in bright, indirect light, not direct sun. Mist the ferns daily and keep them away from drafts and heat sources. Feed blooming plants twice a month with a dilute liquid fertilizer.

Forcing Bulbs Tulips and daffodils can bloom on your windowsill even while winter rages outdoors when you create artificial, shorter seasons. Here are some tips.

- Use a pot twice as tall as bulbs.
- Put in as many bulbs as you can without letting them touch, flat side of tulips out. Set bulb tips even with pot rim. Cover with soil.
- Water, then label pots. Move pots to cold storage.
- Allow 15 weeks from potting to bloom. Most require 12 weeks of cold for rooting, plus 3 weeks at room temperature to flower. (Tulips need 15 weeks for rooting; narcissus, only three.)
- Simulate winter cold and darkness in a refrigerator, cool basement, or garage. Temperatures should be 35–50 degrees Fahrenheit and never below freezing. Keep soil moist.

Gardener's Tip

In a big hurry? Buy ready-to-bloom plants and transplant them into one large container.

■ When stems are an inch or two high and roots are growing through the drainage holes, move to a cool room in your house, away from direct sunlight. When shoots are about 4 inches tall, set pots in a warm, bright area to stimulate blooming. Keep soil moist.

A single pot can display a colorful array of bulbs.

Caring for Houseplants

*K*eeping your plants healthy and happy is a simple matter of knowing how much light, water, and fertilizer they need. Ask questions when you purchase or receive a new plant. Try to provide your plants with growing conditions as nearly perfect as you can— then just sit back and enjoy them.

Container and Soil Savvy

Most houseplants are sold in standard plastic pots with less-than-ideal soil. Give some thought to both before leaving the plant in that condition.

Containers Clay pots have been popular with gardeners for years and work well because they let air in and moisture out. They come in many sizes, including hand-molded shapes. Always soak new clay pots in water overnight before using. Scrub old pots between plantings, or, if disease has been a problem, soak in a bleach solution (1 part bleach to 9 parts water). Rinse.

■ Glazed or plastic pots stay clean more easily than clay pots. They also are cheaper, lighter, and come in more colors. Plants will need fewer waterings, but because these pots let in less air, watering and feeding must be more exact.

■ All containers should have drainage holes in the bottom. If you want to use decorative items like old crocks, put pots with drainage holes inside the crocks. Each pot needs a plastic or clay saucer to collect the excess water.

■ You also can use plastic buckets, milk cartons, window boxes, and such. Use a drill, hot ice pick, or knife to cut a drain hole, if needed.

■ Pots come in a variety of sizes; the width of the opening at the top determines its size.

Soil You can buy potting soil or mix your own. For an all-purpose formula, use one part sand (or perlite or vermiculite), one part peat moss, and two parts loamy garden soil. Sterilize any of the ingredients that could contain weed seeds, insects, or diseases by baking them in a 200° oven for 45 minutes. Purchased potting soils already are sterilized.

Gardener's Tip

A new, unconditioned clay pot tends to draw water out of the soil, robbing the plant. To avoid this, completely immerse the pot in a pail of water. Let stand till all bubbling and hissing stop.

For succulents or African violets, add more sand or peat moss or buy special mixes. Orchids need a special soilless mixture such as fern bark or osmunda fiber.

Whatever you use, be sure the soil is neither powdery dry nor soggy. Store it in a closed plastic bag or container.

Buy premixed potting soil or mix your own. Clockwise from right: vermiculite, sand, black loam, perlite, and peat moss.

Repotting and Potting Up

If a plant is thriving, assume it is happy in its pot. Some plants, though, may need repotting right after you buy them, especially if young and actively growing. Garden-center plants often are root-bound, and the soil used may not be the best.

Taking a plant out of a pot and putting it back in the same-size pot is called repotting. Putting it in a larger pot is called potting up. The technique is similar.

Repotting Do this to improve the soil when the plant is new, or to switch to a more decorative—or different type of—pot. For plants that go dormant, repot at the end of the dormant period, just before the plant's active growing season.

To check the roots, gently knock the plant out of the pot. Healthy white roots should be numerous around the outside of the root ball, but not crowded into a solid mass or winding round and round in a tangle. Pot up if the roots have nowhere left to grow.

Potting Up Young seedlings and cuttings need potting up frequently for growth to continue unchecked. If you notice that growth slows in an older plant or if it wilts too soon after watering, lower leaves turn yellow, or new leaves stay small, it's time to look at the root ball. If you receive a gift planter with several plants crowded together, pot them up soon so they will have room to spread naturally.

Gardener's Tip

The day before repotting or potting up, moisten the soil. This makes it easier to get the plant out and helps shield the plant from the trauma of the change. Soil should be firmly moist, not dry or soggy.

How to Pot Up:

■ Select the new pot, usually one size larger (½ to 1 inch) than the present pot. Put a crockery shard over the bottom hole to keep the soil in the pot. Large pots should have a layer of shards.

■ To loosen the plant, put one hand over the soil and around the stem. Turn the pot over and rap it firmly against a hard surface. The soil and roots usually come out in a compact unit. If they don't, run a knife between the soil and pot to loosen.

■ Keep the root ball as intact as possible, unless the roots have become a snarl. If they're snarled, loosen some of them around the edges and bottom; trim broken or soft roots.

■ Place the plant in the center of the pot with the base of the stem about ½ to 1 inch below the pot rim. Fill with soil around the root ball, burying the plant to the same level. Tap pot; add soil as needed.

■ Water plant immediately. Keep in indirect light until it shows new growth. Keep moist, never soggy.

When potting up, go up one size. If a plant was in a 4-inch pot, use a 5-inch (not 6-inch) pot.

Press added soil firmly around the plant in the new pot. Tap the pot to even the soil and eliminate air pockets. Add more soil.

Lighting Requirements

Proper light is critical for success with houseplants. Check the lists on pages 12 and 13 to find out what kind of light a plant needs before you purchase it. If it needs more than you have available, pass it up until you can provide it with the necessary light through grow-lights or additional windows.

The Directory of Houseplants (pages 40–61) also indicates the ideal lighting conditions.

There are a few general rules, but all have exceptions. For the most part, flowering plants need more light than foliage plants (yet croton, a foliage plant, needs lots of light to keep its vibrant leaf color). Most plants with thick, fleshy leaves need little light (yet cacti and succulents thrive in bright light).

Some plants flower according to how long light is present each day, rather than how intense it is. Christmas cactus, chrysanthemum, kalanchoe, and poinsettia are examples of plants that need short days (long nights) to flower properly.

High light is found in a greenhouse or by a window with a southern or southwestern exposure. This is intense light, as strong as can be found indoors. It also is referred to as full sun.

Medium light refers to direct exposure from an east or west window. Also receiving medium light (or what's called bright indirect) are spots near a filtered southern or southwestern exposure (or some distance from a similar exposure that's unfiltered).

Low light is found near north windows. The light several feet from an east or west window or far from a southern or southwestern exposure (in both cases, often called indirect light) also qualifies as low light. Low light is common in corners and bathrooms; it is not total darkness.

Artificial Light Many houseplants thrive in artificial light. The most inexpensive artificial source is a fluorescent tube.

Too much intense sun (right) caused this peperomia's leaves to be sickly, lifeless, and colorless. Remove the lackluster leaves and move the plant away from direct sun.

Carefully position plants under the light source (as close as 6 inches, never more than 15 inches away). Keep light on for as many as 16 hours a day, depending on your plant. To increase light intensity, use more tubes, add reflectors, or leave lights on longer. Rotate plants regularly.

Flowering plants fail to bud or bloom in poor artificial light. Foliage plants needing more light get tall and spindly; exposed to too much light they're ghostly or faded.

Too little light caused these mature schefflera leaves (above) to turn yellow. New leaves that grow small and spindly also are a sign of low light.

Water and Temperature Tips

Water Although the need for water is obvious, the solution is all too subtle. You can kill your plants with either neglect or kindness.

Always use tepid water. Cold water can slow growth or injure roots. Softened water also is hard on plants. If your water is high in chlorine, let it stand a day uncovered before using it.

The plant's condition often tells you when to water. Use your finger to test the soil surface for moisture. Small pots may need water every day or two. Large ones may go a week between waterings. Check often; experience soon will tell you what to do.

The amount of water, fortunately, is easier to figure than the frequency. Add water until it drains through the hole in the bottom of the pot and shows in the saucer. This ensures that the entire root area receives a thorough soaking. The roots need air, too, so be sure to empty the saucer 20 minutes after watering.

Temperature Just as plants vary in their need for moisture, they also vary in their temperature requirements. Some plants like it cool; others, tropical.

Most houseplants do well in average house temperatures. To encourage best growth, turn the thermostat down at night. Plants like a 10-degree temperature drop after dark, similar to what they experience in nature.

To grow plants that like cool conditions, keep the thermostat between 60 and 70 degrees in the day, lower at night. For plants that like high temperatures, set the thermostat in the 80s during the day and lower at night.

Prevent cold drafts or blasts of hot air near plants; keep plants away from cold windows and radiators in winter.

Summering Plants Most indoor plants take well to a move outdoors for the summer. Do this after all danger of frost has passed. Move plants first into shade, then into indirect light, and finally, if they are full-sun plants, into bright light. This process, known as hardening off, takes about 14 days.

Place houseplants outside in locations that match their indoor light preferences. Water frequently; mist to increase humidity, kill insects, and cleanse. At season's end, spray plants with insecticide before bringing them indoors. Avoid frost damage; better to bring them in too early than too late.

Using a long-spout watering can, pour until water runs out the drainage hole. Let the plant drain, then dump the excess water.

Humidity and Feeding Hints

Humidity Most plants need more humidity than usually is found in a home, especially when the furnace or air conditioner is running. You can ease this problem with a whole-house humidifier, but there are other ways, too.

Frequent misting of the plants will help. So will setting them on trays of pebbles kept wet (but don't let the pots themselves stand in water). Just grouping plants together helps, too.

During weather extremes, when the furnace or air conditioner runs nonstop, you might run a cool vaporizer or put a problem plant in a plastic bag. Make use of places in your home with the highest humidity: the laundry, bathroom, and over the kitchen sink.

Feeding Plants Feeding instructions may seem more confusing than those for watering, but they also are less critical. Buy a good, balanced houseplant fertilizer for most indoor plants, a specialized one if you have many African violets, bromeliads, or orchids.

Read the label. The three numbers (such as 10-20-10) refer to the levels of nitrogen, phosphorus, and potassium. Nitrogen gives the plant lush foliage. Phosphorus keeps roots and stems strong and healthy. Potassium encourages blooms.

Organic fertilizers are blood meal, bonemeal, cow manure, fish emulsion, and kelp products. Chemical fertilizers are sold under a variety of product names, and chemical analysis varies by brand. Read labels.

Water the day before feeding. Fertilizers—most for houseplants come in solution form—can burn if the soil is dry. Getting the solution on the leaves will give them a good foliar feeding; avoid fertilizing the flowers, however, or spotting could result. Follow directions or give less. Never give more.

Plants need little feeding in the winter when they are almost dormant, more in the spring and summer when they are growing more actively.

For plants that have grown large, such as the rubber plant taking over the bedroom or the philodendron covering a window, give the minimum amount of food to purposely keep growth slow.

Do not feed seedlings until they have their first true leaves, and then use a diluted dose. Hold off feeding new or repotted plants for several weeks until they've had time to adjust to their new home. And remember, feeding is seldom the cure for a sick plant.

Keep plants healthy for up to three weeks while you're away by watering them, then covering them with makeshift plastic tents. Use bamboo stakes or bent clothes hangers to support the plastic above the plant leaves.

Houseplant Beauty Cues

Simple little tricks can make a big difference in the appearance of the healthiest plants and perk up the ones with minor ailments.

■ Give your plants a quarter to half turn each week. This will give them nice rounded shapes. Turning also lets you see the other side of your plants and the shades and shapes of leaves and flowers.

■ Take pot in hand and remove the dead leaves that sneak under the lushest foliage. Give the pot a firm tap on a hard surface to settle the roots. Soak the pot in the sink for a half hour to dissolve the salts in the soil (soaking also will moisten the pores of a clay pot).

■ To give shape to plants like philodendron and ivy, wind the long, trailing branches up over the pot in a pleasing pattern, then pin them to the soil at several points with hairpins, bent pipe cleaners, or bent paper clips. Do this every few months. The branches probably will root at these points, giving you a lusher-looking plant.

■ Some plants need to be trimmed into shape. Remember that taking off end growth encourages side branches just below the cut.

■ Help your plants breathe by cleaning their leaves. You can clean many plants quickly under the shower if you have unsoftened water. Wrap plastic bags around the bases to keep the soil in the pots, then wash with lukewarm water at low to medium force. Let the plants drip-dry. If chemical residue in the water leaves white spots, wipe the spots away with a clean, soft cloth.

■ If the weather is warm, set plants outdoors in the rain. Shower large plants with a spray bottle.

■ You can give your plants that florist shine with special sprays or liquids, or with a cloth dipped in milk. But try not to get any of these solutions on the leaf undersides. You might clog the stomata, the leaves' breathing organs.

■ To clean the dust from large, smooth-leaved plants, hold one hand under a leaf and wipe gently with a rag in the other.

■ Use a dry cotton swab, pipe cleaner, or watercolor brush to softly clean hairy-leaved plants, such as African violet and gloxinia.

■ Watch closely for insects, and wash them away with soapy water. Vigilance is the best cure for insect problems. If you use sprays, put the plants in plastic bags to concentrate the effect. Higher humidity also eases plant stress. Systemic insecticides go into the soil and up through the roots to the entire plant to kill insects.

(See the Troubleshooting Guide, pages 62–63, for more help.)

Wash plants often in lukewarm water (above) to rid of dust and insects. Place in sink; let drip-dry.

Prune an indoor tree (right) to give it a pleasing and sturdy shape. Always cut away any dead or broken branches.

Propagating Plants

The easiest, most inexpensive way to add plants to your collection is to propagate those you already have. Multiplying them yourself will give you the added pleasure of watching baby plants grow up. Depending on the plant, methods include seeds, root divisions, runners and offsets, cuttings (leaf, stem, or root), and air layering.

Seeds and Root Division

Seeds are a satisfying way to start many houseplants, including asparagus fern, bromeliads, cacti, coleus, gloxinia, impatiens, and kalanchoe.

Begin with a fine, sterile medium such as potting soil, sand, vermiculite, perlite, or peat moss; cover with ¼ inch of milled sphagnum moss. Sprinkle seeds across the moss surface or into shallow rows.

Mist with water. Cover the tray with glass or plastic; place on a heating pad (the top of the refrigerator also works). Follow lighting instructions on the seed packet. Mist whenever the medium starts to dry.

When seedlings appear, remove the cover and begin watering the surface whenever the soil starts to dry out. Nighttime dampness encourages mold and fungus, so water early in the morning. Turn the pan or pot periodically—or set under grow-lights—to keep plants growing straight, instead of leaning toward the window.

Thin out the seedlings if you plan to keep the plants in the same pot. If not, transplant when the first true pair of leaves appears (it's the second set of leaves) and plant them in their own small pots. Water again; move plants progressively to brighter light. Fertilize mildly—half the suggested amount diluted in water—every two weeks.

Root division is actually the splitting or cutting up of one plant into two or more parts. Almost any plant that grows from several stems in one pot can be divided. This includes peperomias, most ferns, cast-iron plant, creeping Charlie, and prayer plant. Early spring is usually the best time.

To divide a plant, gently knock it out of its container. Remove the root ball and shake off as much soil as you can. Then gently break the root ball apart to see how the roots are growing to determine the way to divide it.

For example, spider plants actually put out new stems and plants next to the original plant,

similar to a sucker or offset. Separate these and repot. The roots of the sprengeri asparagus fern simply build on each other to make one large root ball; cut these apart. Don't be afraid to use a knife; it's better to cleanly sever the roots than to tear them into pieces. Asparagus ferns often have so many roots you must discard some.

Put the divisions into smaller pots. Water thoroughly, and set in indirect light for a week or two while the plant adjusts.

Dividing roots is one way to enlarge your houseplant collection.

Bulbs also are propagated by root division. The amaryllis and oxalis form offsets that can be cut from the parent plant and potted individually. Propagate before new growth starts in the spring. The tuberous begonia and caladium can be propagated by dividing their tubers into two or more parts and potting them separately. Spring is the best time for dividing.

Runners, Tip Cuts, and Stem Cuts

Runners—the small plantlets that form on aerial shoots (such as on spider plants, piggyback plants)—are easy to propagate. Fill a pot with peat-based rooting medium, and pin the plantlet into the medium with a hairpin or bent paper clip, keeping the plantlet moist until it takes root. Then, sever the stem to the parent plant. Rooting this way takes four to five weeks.

Tip Cuttings Propagating houseplants from cuttings is probably the most common method. Do this in the spring. Almost any plant with trailing stems can be multiplied from tip cuttings. Try coleus, wandering Jew, Swedish ivy, and philodendron.

Select a mature, healthy tip of the main stem or side branch; use a sharp knife or blade to cut just below a leaf node (the place where a leaf grows from the stem). The cutting should be several inches long and have four to six healthy leaves. Remove leaves from the bottom of the piece so they won't be buried in the rooting medium; dip the cuttings in a rooting hormone, if you wish.

Many cuttings will root in plain water, but roots grown in water tend to be brittle and fragile; they often break off as you pot the plant. You'll have better luck using a soilless medium, such as perlite, vermiculite, sand, peat moss, or any mixture of these. Equal portions of perlite and peat moss make a good combination.

If you're rooting only two or three cuttings, a small clay pot works well. If you're rooting more, use a clear plastic shoe box or other larger flat, covered container.

Moisten the rooting mixture and poke holes in it with a knife or pencil. Slip the cuttings in and gently firm soil around the stems.

Mist lightly and cover with the lid or encase in a plastic bag and close tightly. Place under fluorescent lights or in indirect light. In several weeks, check to see whether the cuttings have rooted by giving each a gentle tug. If the cutting resists, it should be sufficiently rooted to pot. (There should be an inch or two of roots.) If the cutting isn't sufficiently rooted, return it to the medium.

When rooting runners, pin the plantlet to the medium with a hairpin or bent paper clip

Stem Cuttings New plants can be produced from sections of stem, especially dieffenbachia and dracaena. Stem cuttings should be 4 to 6 inches long and include one or more nodes. Place each stem section in a moist rooting medium, just covering the nodes with soil. Keep moist. In a few weeks, you'll see new growth. Pot when roots are strong.

Root cuttings (2-inch sections of the plant's root) also can be potted in moist rooting medium.

Cuttings from plants with multiple stems are successfully rooted when the tip is 4 to 6 inches long and includes a leaf node.

Leaf Cuttings and Air Layering

Leaf Cuttings Follow the same procedure for rooting leaf cuttings as described for stem cuttings (a leaf stalk rather than the central stem is used). Take leaf cuttings of such plants as peperomia, hoya, begonia, African violet, and many of the succulents.

Simply cut off a mature, healthy leaf at the stem base with a sharp knife and insert it in a moist rooting medium. In several weeks, tiny leaves will push their way up through the soil. When leaves and stems are strong and healthy, sever plantlets from the parent leaf and pot up individually.

If you're rooting only one leaf, especially the woody-stemmed ones, you can put it in a small plastic bag filled with rooting medium. When the leaf has developed strong roots, pot it and watch for new leaves to emerge. When they do, remove and discard the old leaf.

Many leaf cuttings also will root in water. Simply cover a jar or cup of water with aluminum foil, poke holes in it, and insert one or more leaf cuttings.

To root cuttings of snake plant, cut a mature, healthy leaf into 3-inch segments; place upright in a growing medium so half of each section is buried (sections will not root if upside down). In a couple of months, new shoots will form at the side. Remove when roots are sufficiently strong.

Air layering is more a way to revitalize plants than to propagate them. Through air layering, top-heavy, woody-stemmed plants are induced to grow new roots higher up on the stem.

You can air layer schefflera, dieffenbachia, ficus, and dracena species that have lost their bottom leaves. Use a sharp knife to make a cut approximately one-third of the way down the stem. Make an

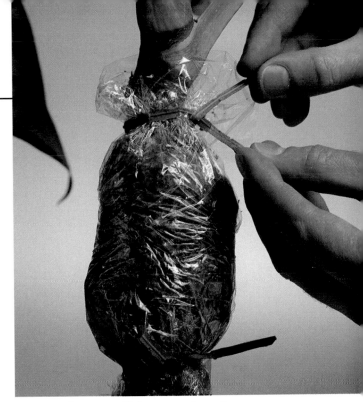

upward slit, cut a notch out of the stem, or just scrape away enough of the bark to expose the plant tissue. Don't cut more than halfway through the stem. If you simply slit the stem, hold the cut open with a toothpick or matchstick.

Next, wrap a baseball-size clump of sphagnum moss around the stem where you've made the cut; wrap with plastic, and secure with wire twists or string.

Periodically check the moss for moisture. If it has dried out, mist lightly and rewrap the plastic. In several weeks (or months, depending on the plant), you'll see roots forming. When they fill the plastic wrap, cut the stem off below the new roots; then plant, moss and all.

Remember you'll be opening the plastic to mist the moss inside.

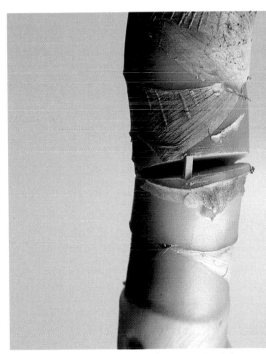

Air layering's critical cut is held open with a wooden pick or matchstick..

Directory of Houseplants

Almost everyone can have green-thumb success with indoor plants when this plant directory is at hand. Both foliage and flowering houseplants are described in considerable detail. You'll also find guidelines on lighting, watering, temperature, and propagation.

Directory of Houseplants

Foliage Plants

ALOE
(Burn plant, first aid plant, medicinal aloe, unguentine cactus)

Aloe sp.

Foliage: Aloe is a succulent with thick, fleshy leaves that thrives in hot, dry conditions. Pluck a leaf, peel away the skin and spines, and use the fluid to treat burns, mosquito bites, diaper rash, and all sorts of minor skin irritations.

Light: Place in bright south windows for best results, although plant will tolerate moderate light. Outside in summer, plant in some shade or move into sun gradually.

Water: Allow to dry between waterings. Water less in winter.

Comments: Allow temperatures to climb to 80s during the day, 10 degrees less at night. Increase plants with offsets. It blooms if the light is bright enough long enough, but seldom indoors.

ARALIA, FALSE
(Threadleaf)

Dizygotheca elegantissima

Foliage: Grows slowly to 5 feet and has delicate, dark green to almost reddish brown leaves arranged like fingers in a fan shape.

Light: Bright indirect light. It will thrive for years with only artificial overhead light. Summer outdoors; stake to protect from wind.

Water: Water thoroughly; keep soil evenly moist.

Comments: Maintain temperatures in low 60s for best growth. Tolerates average temperatures. Use standard potting mix. Feed lightly every 2 weeks during active growth. Propagate by stem cuttings or root divisions.

ASPARAGUS FERN
(Lace fern)

Asparagus setaceus

Foliage: Graceful, lacy foliage often used in hanging baskets.

Light: Place in high light in fall and winter, southeastern exposure in spring and summer.

Water: Keep soil evenly moist. Mist daily to raise humidity.

Comments: Maintain average temperatures but never below 50 at night. Cut back regularly; grows rapidly. Feed monthly during active growth, less rest of the year. Propagate by division.

AVOCADO
(Alligator pear)
Persea americana

Foliage: Grows from the pit of the fruit. When plant gets 6 leaves, cut it back to 2. Also pinch branch tips as they form to keep plants from getting too tall and skinny. Treelike shape.

Light: Place in bright to indirect sun. Grows in full sun outdoors in subtropics.

Water: Let dry between waterings. Good drainage prevents root rot.

Comments: To start, select ripest fruit. Remove and clean pit; let stand in a warm spot overnight. Peel off skin; insert 3 toothpicks around the fattest part of the pit. Rest picks on the edge of a jar so water just covers the flat-bottom end of pit. Pot up when rooted. Seed splits as a tiny stem arises in 4 to 8 weeks, sooner at 85 degrees. Keep seed out of direct sun until growth starts.

BABY'S-TEARS
(Japanese moss, Irish moss)
Helxine soleiroli or Soleirolia soleiroli

Foliage: Slender, horizontal stems, crowded with tiny round leaves; won't grow far over the edge of a pot because they must have contact with the soil.

Light: Bright indirect light.

Water: Even moisture and high humidity.

Comments: Combine baby's-tears only with plants that are fairly thirsty. The leaves resent wetting, and the plant is sensitive to cooking or heating gas. Prefers soil high in peat. Propagate by division.

BOSTON FERN
Nephrolepis exaltata 'bostoniensis'

Foliage: Pale green leaves that can stretch 3 feet.

Light: Medium light of east window.

Water: Allow soil to become dry between thorough waterings. Mist. Raise humidity in warm weather.

Comments: Maintain up to 75-degree temperatures in daytime, no less than 50 at night. Use clay pots and porous soil. Pot up when severely root-bound. Avoid insecticides. Propagate by division in early spring or by runners (threads off side of plant).

CALADIUM
Caladium sp.

Foliage: Intricately marked leaves of white, pink, red, green, silver, and combinations of each. Remove insignificant blooms.

Light: Indoors, place in bright indirect light; outdoors, in shade. Hot sun can scorch leaves.

Water: Water when soil surface is dry. When in full leaf, caladiums can drink a lot. Provide good drainage. They like heat and humidity.

Comments: Start bulbs indoors in April in trays of vermiculite with bottom heat. Repot as they grow. Put outdoors only after the ground is warm and frost danger passes. Lift bulbs and bring inside for winter. Acid soil gives deepest colors. Propagate by bulb divisions.

CAST-IRON PLANT
(Barroom plant)
Aspidistra elatior

Foliage: Long, tapered, dark green or variegated leaves that arise on stems from a crown.

Light: Place near window out of direct sun for most luxuriant look. Will survive in dark corners.

Water: Let dry between soakings. Overwatering causes more problems than neglect.

Comments: Place in areas with temperatures from 45 to 85 degrees. The solid green varieties prefer rich

Cast-Iron Plant

soil. Variegated varieties will revert to all green in rich soil. Too much sun will yellow leaves. Trim off brown leaf tips. Propagate by cutting the root ball apart with a sharp knife.

CHINESE EVERGREEN
(Chinese waterplant, painted drop-tongue, spotted evergreen)
Aglaonema sp.

Foliage: Some varieties grow 15 to 24 inches tall; others grow 3 feet tall. Lance-shape leaves grow on thick stalks. Variegated type requires more light for best dappling.

Light: Place in north window or near center of room.

Water: Keep evenly moist. Plant can grow in water alone; add charcoal to keep water clear and soluble fertilizer occasionally after changing the water completely.

Comments: Needs temperatures in low 80s during the day and no less than the low 60s at night. Use all-purpose soil mixture. Tolerates heat and low humidity. Propagate by root division or stem cuttings.

COLEUS
(Painted nettle, flame nettle, painted leaves)
Coleus sp.

Foliage: Velvety leaves come in reds, greens, yellows, bronze, and chartreuse; leaf edges may be scalloped or ruffled.

Light: Provide bright or indirect light indoors, sun or shade outside. Good on the north or east side of building. Lack of light dulls colors.

Water: Keep evenly moist for lush growth. Leaves will wilt if thirsty; revive with water or evening dew.

Comments: Remove spikes of purple flowers; pinch for bushy growth. Use standard soil mix. Feed once a month during the growing season. Replace old plants with new cuttings once a year, or start from seeds for new colors. Plants will root in water.

CORN PLANT
Dracaena fragrans 'massangeana'

Foliage: Leaves resemble corn leaves, only thicker and darker green with stripes. Stalks will grow very tall, often woody and bare, with a cluster of leaves at the end.

Light: Place in east window or out of direct sun in south or west exposure. Leaf edges will develop brown spots in too much sun.

Water: Keep soil just moist to the touch. Lower leaves may drop off if plant gets too dry.

Comments: Aim for 60- to 75-degree temperatures. Strip lower leaves for accent. Use a loose, humus-rich soil mix with good drainage. Feed every 3 months year-round. Plant 3 in a tub with leaf tops at different heights for drama. Propagate from tip cuttings or pieces of stem with buds, or by air layering. New growth will sprout from stub.

CREEPING CHARLIE
Pilea nummulariifolia

Foliage: Light green leaves on reddish stems; grows well in hanging baskets. (Note: not the same as garden creeping Charlie.)

Light: Bright or indirect sun.

Water: Keep evenly moist.

Comments: Likes average temperatures, 65 to 75 degrees. Add extra peat moss for a rich potting soil. Feed lightly every 2 months; keep humidity high. Pinch leggy growing tips. Propagate by stem cuttings or division.

CROTON
(Garden croton, Joseph's coat, variegated laurel)
Codiaeum sp.

Foliage: Long, waxy leaves are spectacular, with bright colors, patterns, and blotches of yellow, pink, red, and bronze.

Light: Provide strong light at least 4 hours a day, or leaves will revert to green. Colors return if placed outdoors in summer, but harden the plant carefully both going out in summer and coming back in fall.

Water: Keep soil evenly moist. Mist daily to provide humidity.

Comments: Maintain average temperatures; avoid drafts, which cause leaf drop. Use rich potting mixture with good drainage. Feed every other month from early spring through midsummer. Multiply by stem cuttings, or air layer in spring or summer.

DIEFFENBACHIA
(Dumb cane, mother-in-law-plant, tuftroot)
Dieffenbachia sp.

Foliage: Called dumb cane because sap can cause swelling of the tongue and vocal cords and a loss of voice. Aoid putting your fingers near your mouth or eyes. This evergreen grows 6 feet or more in height with a thick trunk and large, patterned 1½-foot leaves that arch gracefully.

Light: Offer north, east, or west light with no more than 2 hours of daily sun. Plant tolerates a wide range of light, but full sun can yellow its foliage.

Water: Let the soil dry on the surface between waterings. Occasionally, immerse pot or move plant to a steamy bathroom.

Comments: This tropical native likes heat—temperatures into the 80s by day, no less than 60s at night. Feed monthly in spring and summer. Expect lower leaves to die. When the leggy stem becomes unsightly, air layer. Also will root in water. A new stem will sprout on the stub, so cut to desired height.

ENGLISH IVY
Hedera helix

Foliage: A hardy ground cover turned houseplant. Train plants on supports for special shapes. Several varieties offer a choice of leaf shapes, sizes, variegations, textures, and habit.

Light: Offer filtered light or a north window.

Water: Keep evenly moist, well drained, and a bit drier in winter.

Comments: Place in cool spots, 55 degrees at night. Shower or mist both sides of leaves weekly to combat mites. Roots in water

FIDDLE-LEAF FIG
Ficus lyrata

Foliage: Shiny, leathery leaves in the shape of a violin.

Light: Place in bright, indirect sun. Full sun can burn this plant.

Water: Water well when soil surface dries. As plant grows, be sure water reaches bottom of pot but does not gather and sit.

Comments: High temperatures for best growth. Use all-purpose potting soil lightened with a little sand or perlite. Feed 3 or 4 times a year unless the plant is growing too fast. Keep the leaves dusted clean. Pinch if you want branching. Propagate with tip cuttings in water or rooting media, or air layer.

JADE PLANT
(Chinese rubber plant)
Crassula argentea

Foliage: A popular succulent with jade-colored, round, fleshy leaves. It easily grows 3 feet or taller.

Light: Place in direct sunlight.

Water: Watch overwatering. Let the soil dry between waterings—it can wait as long as 2 weeks.

Comments: Repot using any soil. Plants usually live for years, even when root-bound. Don't feed plants except lightly in summer, or they may grow too fast. Prune for a more treelike shape. Leaves or tip cuttings root easily. Let them lie exposed for a week to form a callus before inserting in sand or perlite.

Norfolk Island Pine

NORFOLK ISLAND PINE
(Star pine)
Araucaria heterophylla

Foliage: Soft, short needles appear on horizontal branches from the trunk at yearly intervals in tiers of 6. Like an indoor evergreen.

Light: Place in medium light but not direct sunlight indoors or out. If the light is too low, too much space will develop between tiers.

Water: Allow to dry between waterings. Plants tolerate generous watering if drainage is excellent.

Comments: Maintain cool temperatures at night for best growth. Decorate these easy plants as Christmas trees, but avoid heavy or hot bulbs. Repot every 2 or 3 years and top-dress every March. Feed no more than once a month during spring and summer. If needles turn brown, cut off affected branches flush with the trunk. Side cuttings will give a one-sided plant. If plant gets leggy, cut off entire top and root it.

PALMS—GENERAL

Foliage: Palms are dramatic plants that create a lush tropical atmosphere and are easy to grow.

Light: Provide bright light indoors, even a bit of full sun in winter. Outside, filtered shade is best.

Water: Offer even moisture. Palms are not desert plants. Moisture is important to prevent browning. A plant in a 9-inch pot requires 1½ quarts of water each week. Mist often to increase humidity.

Comments: Pots should be deep to give roots enough room. Top-dress yearly. Repot only if so root-bound that water won't soak through. Use a porous, lime-type soil with excellent drainage. Feed a slow-release houseplant food every 3 or 4 months. When plants are near the size you want, feed them just once in the spring. Feed potentially tall or spreading plants less frequently than naturally short ones. Summer outdoors; offer wind protection. Propagation by seeds or offsets is possible, but slow and impractical.

PEPEROMIA
(Many common names, most including the name peperomia)
Peperomia sp.

Foliage: Thick, semisucculent leaves may be smooth, shiny green, two-tone, corrugated, or deeply ridged, with red, pink, or green trailing or upright stems. Emerald-ripple peperomia has deeply ridged and quilted, dark green and brown, almost heart-shape leaves; ivy peperomia has a silver sheen on its round leaves; watermelon peperomia has stripes.

Light: Place in medium to bright light, but not direct sun. A bright north window is fine, but diffuse the sun in other windows.

Water: Allow to dry between waterings during winter. Keep evenly moist during active growth. Likes humidity.

Comments: Keep in warm room, 55 to 75 degrees. Use standard potting mix with added sand or perlite; repot infrequently. Feed no more than once a month during active growth, not at all in winter. Root tip cuttings of branching varieties, leaves of others. Plant just the base of the leaf in the medium. Crowns also can be divided on some peperomias.

PHILODENDRON
Philodendron sp.

Foliage: The most common variety has smooth, 3- to 4-inch heart-shape leaves. Selloum or saddle-leaf philodendron sends up leaves as large as 2 feet long.

Light: Place in bright indirect light; plants will live in low light.

Water: Provide ample water, keeping soil evenly moist. Many types appreciate a support wrapped with moist sphagnum moss. Water sphagnum, too.

Comments: Maintain temperatures in the 80s for best growth. Feed the plants every 3 or 4 months. Large types send out long, ropelike aerial roots; stick into soil or clip off. Large types may form offsets around base that can be separated. Propagate by ground layering, stem cuttings, or seed.

PRAYER PLANT
(Maranta, rabbit's-foot, rabbit's-tracks, ten commandments)
Maranta sp.

Foliage: At night its leaves—oval with intricate texture and color—fold together.

Light: Place in medium to low light. Avoid all but cool morning sun. Lower light intensifies colors.

Water: Keep evenly moist and mist daily. Use tepid water. Leave slightly drier in winter.

Comments: Use high temperatures (80s) for best growth. Use a peat-rich soil mix and feed lightly only during the summer, not more than once a month. In January, trim back the older leaves, or cut stems back to the soil. Propagate by tip cuttings, air layering, division, or seed.

REX BEGONIA
Begonia x rex-cultorum

Foliage: Colored patterns, metallic markings on large leaves.

Light: Medium (bright indirect) light except in fall and winter, then less. Avoid full sun.

Water: Keep soil evenly moist; reduce in fall and winter. Do not mist, but raise humidity.

Comments: Plant rhizomes in shallow pot in peat-rich soil. When growing, feed every 14 days with dilute solution. In fall, let die back. Store in cool, dark spot until February, then water more and bring to light. Propagate by seed or leaf cuttings.

RUBBER PLANT
Ficus elastica

Foliage: A bold tree with large, rubbery leaves on straight stems. Many varieties.

Light: Expose to medium light. Tolerates low light.

Water: Allow soil to dry out between waterings. Mist often; raise humidity.

Comments: High temperatures make for best growth. Tolerates average temperatures. Pot up only when severely root-bound. Use porous soil. Pinch growing tip from young plant for multiple stem growth. Feed every 14 days with mild solution during active growth. Cut stem back to base if plant gets too large or leggy; stump regenerates. Root tip for another plant. Propagate by air layering, tip cuttings, or leaf-bud cuttings.

SCHEFFLERA
(Australian umbrella tree, Queensland umbrella tree, octopus tree)
Brassaia actinophylla

Foliage: The shiny horizontal leaves look like wheels, with 6- to 8-leaflet spokes about 1½ inches wide and 5 to 9 inches long.

Light: Give strong light but not direct sun. Turn plant often.

Water: Let soil surface dry between waterings. More tolerant of low humidity than most plants.

Comments: During the day, likes high temperatures. Tolerates average temperatures. Feed lightly once or twice a year. Multiply by potting any suckers from around base or by air layering.

Directory of Houseplants

SNAKE PLANT
(Sansevieria, hemp plant, or mother-in-law's tongue)
Sansevieria sp.

Foliage: Tall leaves make prime vertical accents in arrangements. The plant also endures where others falter, surviving dim daylight, haphazard watering, heat, dust, and dry air.

Light: Provide bright light, even an east window. Can exist for a long time in dim corners.

Water: Offer low humidity because it is a succulent. Keep soil on the dry side. Water only once every 2 weeks in fall and winter.

Comments: Temperatures in 80s during the day for best growth. Feed no more than once a month and only in spring and summer. Increase by root division or from cuttings of leaf sections. Cuttings of variegated varieties may revert to all green.

SPIDER PLANT
(Airplane plant, ribbon plant, spider ivy)
Chlorophytum comosum

Foliage: Popular and dependable, with long, thin, arching leaves of dark green, often with one or more white stripes down the middle. The stems grow out, produce little white flowers, then plantlets.

Light: Place in bright light, although plant will grow slowly even in a north window. Outdoors, provide shade and wind protection.

Water: Let soil dry, then water and mist generously.

Comments: Maintain temperatures of 60 to 75 degrees. Feed weekly with mild solution to encourage longer leaves and more offspring. Runners will root easily in soil or water before or after separation. Do not feed the runners until they become established. Use standard potting mix.

UMBRELLA PLANT
(Nile grass, umbrella palm, umbrella sedge)
Cyperus alternifolius

Foliage: This plant has feathery top growth that complements the older, coarser foliage. Stiff stems grow from a clump, and palmlike leaves radiate from the top of the stem. Little flowers bloom from June to October and form additional umbrellas above the foliage.

Varieties range from 6 inches to 4 feet tall.

Light: Medium (bright indirect) light except in winter, when high light is better.

Water: Provide constant moisture. Umbrella plant is one of the very few houseplants whose pot can stand in a saucer of water.

Comments: Maintain average temperatures. Feed every 2 weeks during spring and summer. Divide plants or root leaf rosettes.

WANDERING JEW
Tradescantia or Zebrina sp.

Foliage: The two types of wandering Jew are unrelated except in form, but both are no-kill plants with similar red, purple, green, and silver leaf marks, and trailing habit.

Light: Provide full sun to indirect light; the brighter the light, the deeper the colors.

Water: Offer humidity and keep soil evenly moist. Grows in water.

Comments: Maintain average temperatures; avoid cold drafts. Pinch constantly to keep plants from getting leggy, or double the

Wandering Jew

runners back to the soil and pin them down to root. Cuttings root easily at any time.

WEEPING FIG
Ficus benjamina

Foliage: One of the finest indoor trees. Branches weep slightly and have small, shiny leaves.

Light: Medium (bright indirect) light is best; filtered light in summer.

Water: Allow soil to dry between thorough waterings. Mist frequently. Tolerates dry conditions; prefers humidity.

Comments: Average temperatures are fine; avoid cold drafts. Plant gets large; pot up if needed. Feed every 14 days with mild solution. Prune to desired shape in spring. Some leaves yellow and drop off after any move and in winter. Propagate by air layering.

Flowering Plants

ACHIMENES
(Magic flower, monkey-faced pansy, orchid pansy, widow's tears)
Achimenes sp.

Flowers: Showers of colored tubular blooms spring until fall.

Light: Protect from midday sun; likes an east window.

Water: Be sure to keep moist. If it dries, it's instant dormancy.

Comments: For blooming, needs 60-degree night temperatures, up to 80s in daytime. Start rhizomes in moist sphagnum or vermiculite in spring, then transfer several to a pot or hanging basket of half peat and half sand and soil. Feed twice a month during bloom. In late October, decrease water so plants die down naturally. Store unpotted rhizomes in dry sand or vermiculite in 50-degree temperatures until spring. Propagate by stem cuttings in spring, rhizome division when repotting, or seed in winter.

AFRICAN VIOLET
Saintpaulia sp.

Flowers: Flowers come in shades of white and pink to purple, double or single, with rich form variations. Velvety leaves have varied edgings and colors, purple to metallic.

Light: Place in bright indirect (medium) light. East windows are best; north windows in the summer. Plants like artificial light, 14 to 18 hours a day.

Water: Plant in wick-watering pots for best results. Otherwise, water only when soil surface dries. Tepid water in shade will not hurt leaves. Avoid cold water or full sun.

Comments: Maintain high temperatures; keep in warm room, 60 to 75 degrees, day and night. Avoid sudden changes. For humidity, set plants on trays of pebbles; don't mist leaves. Use African violet potting mix, or add peat, perlite, sand, or leaf mold to regular mixes. Feed with an African violet food; dilute some in each watering. Crowns sometimes need dividing. Leaf cuttings usually root easily but rather slowly. Or propagate by seeds or division.

AZALEA
Rhododendron sp.

Flowers: Bright, showy flowers in white or many shades of pink. Will bloom for several weeks indoors.

Light: Give up to 4 hours of direct sunlight daily.

Water: Water generously. After 15 minutes, water again. Or sink whole pots in water for a half hour (never longer).

Comments: Needs cool night temperatures—40 to 65 degrees—to bloom. After bloom, feed with acid fertilizer every 2 weeks until fall, monthly after that. Never feed while in bloom. Summer outdoors in filtered light. Top-dress with acid peat in fall. Water as needed. Propagate by stem cuttings, ground layering, or seed.

BROMELIADS—GENERAL

Flowers: Exotic, stiff leaves and vase-shape trunks with bright, bold, unusual flowers.

Light: Requirements vary. Bright but not full sun for many; others need medium light. The stiffer the leaves, the more light needed.

Water: Keep water in center of cup formed by leaves; water base once a week. Like humidity; don't mist in bright sunlight.

Comments: Plants thrive in commercial soil mix of half fir bark or sphagnum moss, and half sand for good drainage. Roots need little space. Feed little—every 6 to 8 weeks in summer. They form offsets at the base; separate these and pot to multiply stock.

CYCLAMEN
(Poor man's orchid)
Cyclamen persicum

Flowers: Round to heart-shape leaves are mottled and mounded on long, slender stems. It has exquisite blooms with recurved butterfly petals that rise above the foliage in great profusion.

Light: Give bright light to full sun filtered by curtains. Cyclamen also likes artificial light.

Water: Water from the bottom and never get the leaves wet. The succulent stems grow from a corm slightly concaved at the top, and if the corm holds water, rot sets in.

Comments: Maintain temperatures from 50 to 68 during day; drop 10 degrees at night. This need for low temperatures is the reason cyclamen usually doesn't survive indoors for long periods. Discard without guilt when they go. Start from seeds.

CYMBIDIUM
Cymbidium hybrids

Flowers: Stunning orchids in winter; grassy stems.

Light: Place in high light in winter, medium to high light otherwise. Summer outdoors if possible. Needs 3 weeks with 12 hours of darkness in fall for new bloom.

Water: Keep evenly moist, not soggy. Never allow to dry out.

Comments: Maintain average temperatures; needs 55 degrees or below during the 3 weeks of short days prior to blooming. Use special orchid mix. Fertilize with dilute solution while blooming. Propagate by division, leaving parent plant with 4 stems.

FUCHSIA
(Lady's-eardrops)
Fuchsia sp.

Flowers: The long, pendent blooms have recurved petals about halfway down, then a bell skirt bottom from which the stamens and pistil extend.

Light: Provide bright light, but protect from midday sun. East or west windows are best.

Water: Keep soil evenly moist, not soggy. Plants have shallow roots.

Comments: Keep your house cool at night, 50 to 65 degrees. It will perish in overheated rooms. Feed twice a month when flowering. Reduce both water and food between blooming periods. Pinch to keep bushy. Propagate from stem cuttings.

Upright or trailing, fuchsia produces spectacular bell-like blooms in a wide range of colors.

GARDENIA
(Cape jasmine)
Gardenia jasminoides

Flowers: Shiny-leaved plants with delicate, wildly fragrant flowers, often difficult to grow.

Light: Place in sun in winter, bright shade in summer.

Water: Water heavily. Gardenias can sit with water always in the saucer. Mist plants daily.

Comments: Maintain temperatures in the low 60s to bud, not below 70 once they form. If you buy a plant in bud, remove all but a very few.

Repot every spring in a porous, peat-rich (by half), acid (no lime) soil mix. Feed with special acid food. Put plants outdoors in summer with pots sunk to the rim for constant moisture. Pinch flower buds to encourage winter bloom. Propagate by cuttings or seed.

GLOXINIA
Sinningia sp.

Flowers: Huge, scallop-edge, velvetlike trumpets. They bloom—often white on the outside and edged with brilliant color inside—above a low mound of large leaves.

Light: Offer bright light but not direct sunlight. Too little light creates leggy stems.

Water: Keep soil evenly moist, but avoid waterlogging. Keep water off the hairy foliage and the top of the tuber by watering around the edge of the pot or from the bottom.

Comments: Likes high temperaures and humidity except during dormancy. Use African violet soil mix. At dormancy, store in dark place at 50 degrees; repot when growth begins. Feed lightly every few weeks beginning as soon as flower buds develop. Start new plants from seed, or root leaf cuttings at the base, bracing leaves with sticks.

HIBISCUS
(Chinese hibiscus, Chinese rose)
Hibiscus sp.

Flowers: The showy blooms come in bright shades of red, pink, purple, orange, yellow, and white, and are 4 to 8 inches across. Each one lasts only a day and stays lovely even without water.

Light: Provide full sun for bloom. Even without flowers, hibiscus is an attractive foliage plant.

Water: Keep soil evenly moist when plant is in flower, on the dry side at other times. Likes humidity.

Comments: Keep plants in a warm spot when growing and blooming, a cool place at other times. In March, before new growth starts, prune plants back by half and repot if necessary. Use a standard potting soil and feed lightly only when in growth or bloom. Pinch tips to keep plants compact and bushy. Summer plants outdoors for maximum

bloom in the summer and fall. Propagate by seed or tip cuttings from new growth.

KALANCHOE
(Aurora borealis plant, Christmas kalanchoe)
Kalanchoe blossfeldiana

Flowers: In full sunlight, kalanchoe's leaf edges are reddish, and bright clusters of tiny flowers bloom for long periods. Flowers form only when days are short, so the plant will not bloom if it gets any night light at all.

Light: Give full sun in spring, fall, and winter. Avoid direct sun during the hottest part of day in summer.

Water: Let soil dry between waterings. Water more frequently until the flowers fade, then keep soil on the dry side for a month or two with just enough moisture to keep the leaves from shriveling.

Comments: Place where nights are cool, down to 50 degrees. Prune well back after flowers fade, then put in shade outside. Bring back to a sunny window in September, or take stem or leaf cuttings for new plants.

LADY'S-SLIPPER
(Slipper orchid)
Paphiopedilum sp.

Flowers: Tricky to grow, produces pouchlike blooms once a year.

Light: High light in winter; medium (bright indirect) the rest of the year. Eastern exposure is best.

Water: Keep growing medium constantly moist and humidity high. Don't let plant become dry.

Comments: Maintain average temperatures. Drop by 10 degrees at night. Use orchid potting mix and shallow pot; repot yearly to change medium. Feed every 14 days in spring and summer; monthly in fall and winter. Propagate by division or seed.

POINSETTIA
Euphorbia pulcherrima

Flowers: Bright red, pink, or white colors in large showy blooms.

Light: Provide bright light until plant reaches peak of bloom, when it can survive with less. Avoid drafts. Most important: enjoy the plant. Place it accordingly.

Water: Be sure both the pot and any foil or paper wrapping allow drainage. Water enough to drain through, then check plant daily and water again when the surface begins to dry.

Comments: Place plants in a cool room, especially at night. Feed within 10 days after purchase. Feed monthly after that. Poinsettias root from stem cuttings and grow easily, but they will not form buds unless they have 12 to 14 hours of complete darkness each day.

SPATHIPHYLLUM
(White anthurium, peace lily, spathe flower)
Spathiphyllum sp.

Flowers: Foliage looks much like smaller aspidistra; sword-shape leaves grow 1½ feet long. The pale green sheath turns white as it opens. The true flowers are tiny and surround a slender protruding stalk. Each bloom lasts for weeks, usually in January and February.

Light: Provide bright light in winter, diffused light in summer. Plants will bloom in shade, but with sparse, undersize flowers.

Water: Keep soil evenly moist. Increase humidity.

Comments: Place in a warm room. Feed every 2 months from March to September. Divide the roots of pot-bound plants after flowering. Pot up each spring. When leaf tips yellow, check for too much or not enough water, or insufficient food.

SUCCULENTS— GENERAL

Flowers: The unique forms and sculpted shapes result partly from stored water.

Light: Place most succulents in south windows. Some need protection from intense afternoon sun. When you move them outdoors for the summer, ease them into sun or open shade gradually; otherwise, they will cook in their own juices and turn transparent.

Water: During fall and winter, water only enough to keep the roots and soil from drying, not enough to encourage new growth. The plants will take considerably more water during their active growing and blooming time, in spring and summer. Be sure their pots provide drainage; water every other week.

Comments: Leaves fall off at the slightest pressure. Pot with a layer of drainage in the bottom, preferably gravel, broken pottery, or similar jagged-edge material. Buy potting mix for cactus and succulents. Leave an inch at the top of the pot. Feed succulents frequently but lightly. Succulents multiply easily from cuttings, seeds, grafts, or offsets.

TUBEROUS BEGONIA
Begonia x tuberhybrida

Flowers: Spectacular blooms in many sizes, shapes, and colors.

Light: Expose to medium light during active growth, dark during dormancy.

Water: Keep constantly moist during active growth. Water less after foliage starts to yellow. Stop during dormancy. Raise humidity.

Tuberous Begonia

Comments: Plant tubers, hollow side up and barely exposed, in shallow pots; use soil high in organic matter. Keep moist and at 70 degrees to spur growth. Water and feed regularly. Water less after blooms fade; store clean, dry in cool, dry, dark place. Propagate by cutting shoots off tubers. Use as tip cuttings.

WAX PLANT
(Hoya, hindu-rope, honey plant)
Hoya sp.

Flowers: A dozen varieties, all attractive as foliage plants with thick, succulent, waxlike leaves of varied markings. The clusters of star-shape, fragrant flowers are creamy velvet with a perfect dark pink star in the center, blue-white with red centers, or yellow-green.

Light: Give bright light, up to 4 hours of sun a day. Lives for years, unblooming, in shade.

Water: Water generously during bloom. Keep almost dry otherwise.

Comments: Average temperatures when active, low 60s in dormancy. Feed every second month. Use extra-rich soil with sand and leaf mold. Tie plants to supports for best growth. Keep plants pot-bound for many flowers. Never remove a stub where the flowers appear or you will be cutting off the next blooms. Propagate with tip cuttings.

Troubleshooting Guide

First Aid for Plants

Symptom: Leaf tips turn brown; lower leaves turn yellow and drop off. Stems get soft and mushy, then turn brown. Soil is soggy, and slimy scum forms on edges of pots.

Cause & Cure: Too much water. Allow soil to dry completely before watering again. Repot if soil is soggy. Make sure plant has adequate drainage. Don't let it sit in water in saucer. Water less often.

Symptom: Leaf tips turn yellow, then turn brown and dry up. Bottom leaves turn yellow.

Cause & Cure: Too little water. Water plant thoroughly by immersing the whole pot in water. Let excess drain away. Water on a strict schedule.

Symptom: Leaves look faded or have yellow or brown "burned" spots. Foliage plants turn brown.

Cause & Cure: Too much light. Move plant out of bright light. Ease up on artificial light.

Symptom: Plant develops long, spindly stems. New growth is weak and pale; leaves are undersize.

Cause & Cure: Too little light. Move plant to a location that gets more light, or supplement natural light with artificial light.

Symptom: Plant grows quickly, but new growth is weak and spindly or streaked with yellow. A crusty scum may form on pots.

Cause & Cure: Too much fertilizer. Flush fertilizer buildup out of the soil and off pot rims by watering the plant several times an hour with tepid water. Let excess moisture run out the bottom. Stop fertilizing for a while, and reduce dosage or frequency.

Symptom: Leaves look yellow but veins are green. New growth is weak and droopy.

Cause & Cure: Too little fertilizer. Set up a fertilizing schedule based on plant's needs and the season.

Symptom: Edges of leaves curl under and turn crispy and brown.

Cause & Cure: Too little humidity or temperature is too high—or both. Add humidity to the air by misting plants or installing a home humidifier. Move to a cooler spot.

Houseplant Pests

Mealybugs These white cottony blobs are apt to be your worst headache. They're sometimes hard to eradicate because they're protected by a water-resistant wax. Dab each bug with a cotton swab dipped in rubbing alcohol, and rinse leaves with clear, cool water. Or use a houseplant miticide, and rinse plants when mealybugs are eradicated.

If you have African violet, fuchsia, coleus, and wax vine, be on the alert. Regular cleanings help prevent outbreak.

Red Spider Mites These tiny bugs feed on the undersides of leaves, spinning fine webs along veins and leaves. They give a plant a rusty look in the early stages, and a gray webby look with anemic foliage later on. Look for them on azalea, hydrangea, and ivy.

If possible, take plant outside and flush bottoms of leaves with a light spray from a garden hose. Or mix a mild soap (not detergent) into a pan of lukewarm water, producing a lather. Cover the top of the pot with foil to hold the dirt, upend the plant, and swish the foliage through the suds. Rinse well with clear water. Follow this procedure once a week until pests are gone. If you use a miticide, wash the leaves to remove the webs.

Scale Scale looks like little green or brown ovals. Scales line up along the main veins of the plant and cause it to lose color, yellow, and die. Prime targets are ferns, palms, and rubber plants.

Gently scrape the scale off with a soft toothbrush or your fingernail. Wash the plant with lukewarm, soapy water.

Aphids These greenish white or black insects cluster in the open where they're easily detected.

Use the tepid, soapy water wash and clear rinse recommended for red spider mites. Or spray with a miticide and rinse when pests have been eradicated.

At least once a year give your houseplants and their pots a thorough housecleaning. Throw out sickly plants before their ailments spread to healthy ones.

Index

THE
NORDSTROM
WAY *to*
CUSTOMER SERVICE
EXCELLENCE

THE HANDBOOK FOR BECOMING THE
"NORDSTROM" OF YOUR INDUSTRY

SECOND EDITION

ROBERT SPECTOR
PATRICK MCCARTHY

WILEY

John Wiley & Sons, Inc.

Library of Congress Cataloging-in-Publication Data:

Spector, Robert, 1947–

The Nordstrom way to customer service excellence : the handbook for becoming the "Nordstrom" of your industry / Robert Spector, Patrick McCarthy. — 2nd ed.
   p. cm.
Includes index.
   ISBN 978-1-118-07667-5 (pbk); ISBN 978-1-118-22266-9 (ebk); ISBN 978-1-118-23653-6 (ebk);
   ISBN 978-1-118-24309-1 (ebk)
1. Customer services—United States—Handbooks, manuals, etc.   2. Nordstrom (Firm)—Management.
3. Department stores—United States—Management.   I. McCarthy, Patrick D. II. Title.
HF5415.5.S626785   2012
658.8'12—dc23   2011039735

Printed in the United States of America

10 9 8 7

In loving memory of my parents,
Fred and Florence Spector,
who taught me The Spector Way:
Work hard, be good, do well.

R. S.

In memory of Ray Black,
who first showed me The Nordstrom Way

P. McC.

Contents

Introduction

This is not a book about selling shoes or clothes or cosmetics or jewelry.

This is a book about creating a corporate culture that encourages, motivates, and compensates your employees to consistently deliver a superior customer service experience for your customers.

Customer service is like the weather. Everybody talks about it but nobody (well, almost nobody) does anything about it.

And yet each one of us is an expert on customer service. At one point or another during the course of our day, we are all customers. We know good service when we see it, and we know bad service when we see it. You don't have to read a book to have it explained to you.

Picture a metaphorical customer service counter. On one side of the customer service counter is you, the customer. You know exactly what your expectations are: a good product or service at a fair price. If there's a problem, you want it taken care of as quickly, seamlessly, and painlessly as possible. Simple stuff. We all know this.

So, then, why is good customer service so rare?

Because a funny thing happens to people when they are on the other side of the customer service counter or the front desk or the reception area or on the the other end of the telephone or Internet—when they are in the position of having to *give* service as opposed to receiving service. Most often, their only concerns are the rules, the process, the manual, the bureaucracy, the way it's always been done. It is as if they hit the "delete" button on their customer service memory. They forget about the Golden Rule, about empathy, about the customer.

You've heard all the excuses: "Sorry, that's against our policy." "Sorry, we have a rule against that." "Sorry, my manager's off today. Can I get an answer to you next week?"

We customers don't ask for much. We want to be taken care of. We want to do business with a company that's going to make our life easier. Most companies, large and small, are based on a business model that is set up to make life easier for the company, not for the customer. That's where Nordstrom comes in. Nordstrom people will do whatever it takes (within reason, of course) to take care of the customer.

"We don't determine what good service is; the customer does," wrote Blake, Peter, and Erik Nordstrom in the employee newsletter, *Loop*. "When you hear the many amazing customer service stories taking place on our selling floor, the one thing they share in common is a spirit of doing what's right for the customer. From the sales floor to support, no matter where we work, our challenge is to constantly put the customer at the center of everything we do. If something is important to the customer, find a way to deliver. If it's not, we need to question if it's worth our time and focus."

Nordstrom urges new employees to be kind. Nordstrom management still believes that the Golden Rule has merit. Management empowers its employees to treat others as they would want to be treated. Nordstrom believes that great service begins with showing courtesy to everyone—customers, employees, and vendors.

Becoming the Nordstrom of Your Industry

When *The Nordstrom Way* was first published in 1995, it struck a chord with many companies in a variety of industries. Several hundred thousand copies and six iterations later, it continues to serve as an inspiration for many different types of businesses.

Although more than 110 years old, Nordstrom continues to be the standard against which other companies and organizations privately (and often publicly) measure themselves.

Nordstrom has long been a popular subject for study among authors of customer service books and educators at business graduate schools such as Harvard and Wharton. *Roll Call*, the newspaper of Capitol Hill, once advised press aides for U.S. congressmen to use the "Nordstrom approach" when trying to sell producers of political talk shows on the benefits of booking their bosses. The *New York Times Magazine* once quoted a minister in Bel Air, California, who told his congregation in a Sunday sermon that Nordstrom "carries out the call of the gospel in ways more consistent and caring than we sometimes do in the church."

In an article in Nashville's newspaper *The Tennessean*, a writer called for local schools to produce a "customer-centric culture," to create "the loyalty and enthusiasm that is crucial to participation, funding, and community pride. The Wal-Mart model is good for some things, but if it is quality you desire, Nordstrom is the way."

Businesses of every kind strive to become the "the Nordstrom" of their industry. Recreational Equipment Inc. has been called "the Nordstrom of sporting goods stores" and *Specialty Foods* magazine described A Southern Season, a store in Chapel Hill, North Carolina, as "the Nordstrom of specialty food."

A top broker for Century 21 once told *Fast Company*, "I want people to think of me as the Nordstrom of real estate."

A dean at Fullerton College in California vowed to create "the Nordstrom of Admissions and Records."

University of Colorado Hospital installed a baby grand piano in the lobby and began advertising itself as "The Nordstrom of Hospitals."

You can find similar comparisons in yoga videos, office furniture, public libraries, construction supply distribution, hot tubs, dental offices, pet stores, sex shops, thermal rolls, foundries, workplace giving, doors and windows, and contract consulting.

I've even found "the Nordstrom of garbage collection." I don't know what its return policy is, and I don't want to find out.

Even Nordstrom uses this metaphor. In describing the company's Rack division of clearance stores, Blake Nordstrom once said, "We like to think that the Rack is the Nordstrom of the discount world."

So what does it mean to be the Nordstrom of your industry? It's not just a smiling face that greets you when you enter the department. It's covering every aspect of the business—the things the customers see and the things that they don't see.

How can an organization create a culture and atmosphere to provide "Nordstrom-like" service? This book answers those questions and shows you how to do it.

A Family Business; a Public Company _____

The old saying about family businesses goes like this: The first generation builds them, the second generation enjoys them, and the third generation destroys them. No one even bothers to mention the fourth generation because there are so few businesses that last that long.

If there was ever a family business that defies that stereotype, it is Nordstrom. Technically, Nordstrom is not a family business. It's been a publicly traded company for more than four decades—over a third of the company's history. The chairman of its board of directors since 2006, Enrique "Rick" Hernandez is not a family member and has never worked for the company. Hernandez who is president and CEO of Inter-Con Security Systems, Inc. of Pasadena, California, heads an outside board that consists of 12 directors, not one of whom has a high national profile, but several have impeccable retail credentials.

Nevertheless, Nordstrom is a family company in the sense that it is still run by members of the family. Brothers Blake, Peter, and Erik (who are on the board of directors) are the fourth generation to work in the business, which was founded by their great-grandfather, John W. Nordstrom. The large extended Nordstrom family—most of whom are not active in the company—owns about 20 percent of the outstanding shares.

Dollar for dollar, Nordstrom is one of the greatest stories in the history of American business. We will never see the likes of it again.

Nordstrom has been ranked among *Fortune* magazine's "100 Best Companies to Work For in America" every year since the list was first published in 1998. In the most recent survey, Nordstrom was the fifth oldest firm, trailing only Goldman Sachs, American Express, S.C. Johnson, and Mercedes-Benz. It is also one of the 25 most-admired companies in the United States, according to *Fortune*.

Blake, Peter, and Erik have carried on the family tradition by always staying current. The Nordstroms profess to not being the smartest guys in the room, but they are certainly as competitive as any other guy in the room. They like to win.

First and foremost, Nordstrom follows a strategy built around the customer—not around price, process, brand, technology, or any other corporate tactic or buzzword you can think of. When the company considers how it can improve service and results, it asks itself one question: "What would the customer want?"

Everything Nordstrom does, every aspect of its business, is seen through the lens of the customer, with the goal of improving the experience that a customer has with Nordstrom. If it matters to the customer, doing it well is good customer service. That's why customer service is the number-one priority. That's why the focus on the customer is emphasized and reemphasized and re-reemphasized at each and every opportunity—including its annual report to shareholders, which always opens with this salutation: "Dear Customers, Employees and Shareholders." Note the order of importance. Nordstrom believes that taking care of the customers and employees ultimately benefits the shareholders (which include management, employees, and customers).

This singular focus on its customers keeps the company disciplined, yet daring, especially in difficult financial times.

When faced with the economic downturn that began in 2007, rapid, firm, methodical decision making allowed Nordstrom to both rein in costs and take advantage of opportunities given to the company by their irresolute competitors. Nordstrom stayed directed toward improving the customer experience. Customers were not going to change for Nordstrom; Nordstrom had to change for the customers.

The company encouraged its entrepreneurial employees to become even more involved in how the business was run. Salespeople were challenged to become more creative with selling methods and to share their successes and failures with their teams. Everyone in the organization was asked for ideas on how to cut down on expenses without cutting down on service.

"We don't have one person whose role it is to maintain the culture or manage service or our reputation," says Blake. "We believe we are all responsible for keeping these components of who we are alive and well at Nordstrom. . . . Personal ownership by all of our people has led to our success and our company's ability to persevere even through the toughest of times."

Nordstrom's Reputation

Nordstrom's reputation for service has evolved through a process that spans the history of the company. Why have they emphasized service? Over the years, they've learned that the more service they've provided the better their business became. It's as simple as that.

Nordstrom creates an emotional experience of shopping through personal service, special customer-focused events, a loyalty rewards program, and a virtually unconditional return policy. Its high-cost, high-touch, high-tech model is famous throughout the world.

What's fascinating is that Nordstrom does not promote its service to the outside world. The company never runs advertisements boasting about its customer service, nor does it ever send out press releases boasting about its customer service. Top company executives rarely comment on service to the press. Yet their reputation has spread throughout the world. We have spoken about the company in a couple of dozen countries in every part of the world. Even people in Caracas or Mumbai or London, who have never set foot in a Nordstrom store, are aware that Nordstrom is known for its service.

How have these people learned about Nordstrom's culture of service? The answer is simple: word of mouth, which is the most powerful advertising of all.

With the exception of Nordstrom, the great department stores of America are no longer controlled or operated by the descendants of the founding merchants.

"Instead of being customer-focused, it's more being customer-driven," says Blake. "This is a subtle yet profound shift. It means putting the customer in the driver's seat and setting aside our own notions and historical preconceptions of how the customer wants to be served. It's about empowering the customer to dictate his or her terms to us when it comes to all the different ways he or she chooses to shop. This puts the customer more squarely in our decisions and how we allocate resources. This is particularly important given the extraordinary speed with which the shopping experience is changing and how customers are rethinking what service is all about. Customers want to do business with those retailers who understand their needs and desires and are moving at their speed. They are responding favorably to those retailers who are mobile, connected, convenient to shop with, and know them regardless of channel."

Nordstrom's number-one goal every year is to improve its customer service. Yes, even Nordstrom believes there is always room to get better.

"It would be easy to accomplish that goal if there were a secret formula to make it happen, but fortunately there is no secret formula," says Blake. "Otherwise, many of our competitors would have discovered and adopted it."

The Nordstroms are a modest bunch. "We don't profess to say that we're the experts in customer service," says Blake, the eldest of three brothers in the fourth generation who have run the company since 2000.

When you discuss customer service with members of the Nordstrom family, they frequently use a word that one rarely hears in American business—humble. They believe that service requires employees to put themselves in the shoes of the customer.

"You need to be humble to do service," said Erik, Blake's younger brother. "The moment you think you're really good at it is when you're not really good at it. If you are connected to the customer, the customer keeps you humble because we're not perfect at it. If you are really looking to the customer, if you're really sensitive to the customer, and sensitive to the people on the front line, you are aware of your shortcomings. That keeps us focused on the things that are necessary in order to give customer service."

Customers have more information and choices than ever before. They have better tools and higher expectations. This changing landscape gives Nordstrom wide-ranging opportunities to combine new tools and techniques with its culture of service to offer a highly personalized customer experience that adapts to customers' changing expectations.

Because Nordstrom's reputation is centered on customer service, its future success is determined by customer service. The company's leaders view their main job as creating an environment where people use their best judgment to take care of the customers.

Is customer service quantifiable? People often ask what kind of metrics Nordstrom uses to measure the effectiveness of their customer service strategy. The answer: "Are sales up or down?" Customers vote with their hard-earned dollars. As they say at Nordstrom, "Sales are the truth."

What Makes Nordstrom Unique?

Nordstrom's business is comprised of people, product, and place. The company combines superior merchandise and motivated people to create an experience for customers that exceeds their expectations. Customers have a myriad of choices to buy apparel, footwear, cosmetics, and accessories. When they shop with Nordstrom, that's the ultimate endorsement.

The chain, which is geared toward middle-to-upper income women and men, offers attractive stores, with a large, varied, and competitively priced inventory of shoes, apparel, accessories, and cosmetics, and a liberal return policy. But many stores do that—at least to varying degrees.

It's got an easy-to-use website and an active, creative social media presence. Again, a lot of companies can say that.

What makes Nordstrom unique is its culture of motivated, empowered employees, each with an entrepreneurial spirit.

Nordstrom encourages, preaches, demands, and expects individual initiative from these people who are on the front lines. These men and women have the freedom to create their own individual businesses. Each of them is a franchise within a franchise. They are empowered to give great customer service. The best Nordstrom sales associates will do virtually everything they can to make sure a shopper leaves the store a satisfied customer.

The simplest explanation for what makes Nordstrom Nordstrom is that their salespeople put themselves in the shoes of the customer. They do whatever they can to make life easier for their customers.

The competition in the retail world can only look on in awe.

Michael Gould, Chief Executive Officer of Bloomingdale's, told *Women's Wear Daily* that, according to a survey of Bloomie's customers, "people expected our service levels to be at parity to Neiman's and Saks, but they didn't expect us to be as good as Nordstrom."

When asked if Bloomingdale's service could ever be as good as Nordstrom's, Gould responded: "Yes. It's a goal. Nothing happens overnight. They are terrific. They have created a mind-set and a perception. The thing that impresses me about Nordstrom and its service is the consistency. We have a lot of instances of great service, but they are consistently at a very high level."

Some rivals of Nordstrom make feeble attempts to emulate the customer service culture. Macy's created a training program called "Magic Selling," where new salespeople were required to go through a three-and-a-half-hour session when they started at the company. Under the old training program, they had to sit through a 90-minute interactive video in a booth. Magic Selling also included seasonal refresher courses and coaching from managers while they were on the sales floor. Salespeople were encouraged to give customers options and advice on purchases, and to make natural connections with shoppers. Sounds nice, but it's just not that simple.

Have you ever seen a book touting Macy's customer service?

Becoming the Nordstrom of Your Industry

This book is divided into three sections.

Phase I deals with *Culture*, because Nordstrom is a culture story. We will look at the company's history because if you don't know the history, you don't know the company. The elements of the Nordstrom

Way were instituted back in 1901 and have been adjusted, refined, and expanded ever since.

We will look at the kind of people who Nordstrom hires, and how they are trained, empowered, mentored, supported, praised, and recognized. We will examine the fascinating paradox of Nordstrom, which offers employees a level playing field to advance their personal and corporate goals, but at the same time encourages both individual achievement and loyalty to the team. And finally, the culture section looks at the company's commitment to corporate social responsibility, from green initiatives to community outreach.

Phase II is about the *Nordstrom Experience*. We will look at every detail that creates the Nordstrom customer experience, including the brick-and-mortar stores, Nordstrom.com, social media, and the personal relationship that customers have with Nordstrom salespeople.

Phase III: *Applications* presents training exercises and activities that will help your company or organization to be the Nordstrom of your particular industry. The idea is to figure out what works for your company in your particular industry and then to put those ideas in motion—every day, every year, from now on.

One caveat: If you truly want your organization to become the Nordstrom of your industry, you must be totally committed for the long haul. If you are not "all in" with this process (which is not as simple as it looks), then don't bother; it's a waste of your time and money. In that case, please pass this book on to someone else.

—Robert Spector

PHASE I

CULTURE

Tell the Story

How Nordstrom Became Nordstrom

Eyes may be the windows to the soul, but shoes are the gateway to the psyche.

—Linda O'Keefe, Shoes

John W. Nordstrom, like the founders of most of America's retail dynasties, was an immigrant. The middle child of five, Nordstrom was born February 15, 1871, in the town of Lulea, in the northernmost part of Sweden, 60 miles below the Arctic Circle. His father, a blacksmith, wagon maker, and part-time farmer, passed away when John (born Johan) was eight years old. By the time he was 11, his mother had taken him out of school so he could work on the family farm.

His life in Sweden, by his own admission, was an unhappy one. As he got older, "My mother seemed to think I was a man, and often remarked that at my age my brother [10 years his senior] could do nearly anything and why couldn't I," he wrote. "I often cried when I had trouble doing things she expected me to do and couldn't, and felt very helpless."

The winter he turned 16 (1887), John decided to leave home and cast his lot in America. With 450 crowns (about $112) of his modest inheritance, given to him by his guardian, he bought a suit of clothes. "The first clothes I ever on my back that were not homespun and handwoven."

His eventual destination was the Pacific Northwest of America, where thousands of Swedes thrived as fishermen, loggers, blacksmiths, shipwrights, and millwrights in a climate and landscape similar to their homeland. Others helped finish the transcontinental railroad. "Give me enough Swedes," proclaimed James J. Hill, the driving force behind the Great Northern Railroad, "and I'll build a railroad right through hell."

There were no railroads in northern Sweden, so John and two young friends began their odyssey with a two-day boat trip to Stockholm, followed by a three-day voyage across Sweden, through the Gota Canal, to Gothenburg, then on to Hull, in northeast England. The first train rides of John's life brought him to Liverpool, where he took steerage passage for the 10-day voyage to Ellis Island, New York. From there, Nordstrom and his friends, unable to speak a word of English, took a train to Stambaugh, Michigan, where he had a cousin and prospects for work.

When he arrived in Michigan, Nordstrom (who had five dollars in his pocket) took a job hauling iron ore with a wheelbarrow, carting it about a hundred feet to a platform and dumping it into railroad cars. For the next five years, his strong back and fierce determination carried him westward through a series of hardscrabble manual labor jobs: logging in Michigan, digging coal in Iowa, mining gold and silver in Colorado, loading railroad ties and carting bricks in Mendocino County, California, and logging Douglas fir trees in Washington state. By the summer of 1896, Nordstrom had saved enough money to buy 20 acres of bottomland for potato farming in the Swedish immigrant enclave of Arlington, Washington, about 50 miles north of Seattle.

Seattle: City of Opportunity

Seattle in the 1890s was "young, raw, and crude," wrote Roger Sale in *Seattle, Past to Present*. White settlers first reached the region in 1852. In 1860, a group of about 150 pioneers settled there. (By way of comparison, New York City in the 1850s already had paved streets and a store named R. H. Macy.) "They didn't come looking for paradise," said one wag. "They came for cheap real estate."

From 1879 to 1890, the city's population rocketed from 1,107 to 43,487, fueled by constant rumors that Seattle would be the terminus of the transcontinental railroad. The nascent city provided equal opportunity for God-fearing pioneers, entrepreneurial visionaries, scam artists, and ladies of the evening. In the book *Sons of the Profits*, an irreverent account of those times, William C. Speidel, the city's iconoclastic historian, wrote that the essence of the "Seattle Spirit" was "enlightened self-interest"—a business philosophy that exists today in Seattle companies such as Starbucks, Amazon.com, and Microsoft.

The mood was feverish. With Seattle about to be connected by rail via the Great Northern Railroad to the rest of North America, making money was on everyone's mind. A leading banker of that era, N. B. Coffman, described the 1890s as a time "of adventure and wild-cat speculation . . . such can never again be witnessed." Norman H. Clark wrote in *Washington: A Bicentennial History*: "There had been nothing like it in American history since the opening of the Louisiana Territory—golden years where no personal ambition, however grandiose, seemed at all unreasonable, when it seemed that every venture might prosper and every family might share in the nobility of wealth because of the democracy of profit."

At breakfast on Sunday morning, July 18, 1897, John Nordstrom picked up a copy of the *Seattle Post-Intelligencer* to see splashed across the front page, in huge capital letters, the magic word: "GOLD!" Coarse gold had been found in the fields of the Klondike, in Canada's Yukon Territory. Five thousand people greeted the steamer *Portland* when it arrived on July 17 at the Seattle waterfront with a much-ballyhooed cargo—"a ton of gold." Coupled with the arrival in San Francisco of the *Excelsior*, with another heavy cargo of gold, the news ignited the world.

John read the story "over and over again . . . discussing this big news," he recalled in his memoir. "Finally I slammed the paper down on the table and said, 'I'm going to Alaska!'" Nordstrom gathered his belongings and "what little money I had and by four o'clock that afternoon I was on the train bound for Seattle and a new adventure."

Arriving at the Seattle waterfront early the following morning, he found a virtually endless line of people waiting to buy tickets for Alaska.

When the coal freighter *Willamette* steamed out of Elliott Bay, heading north for the Inland Passage, it was burdened with 1,200 men, 600 horses, 600 mules, and John Nordstrom. Because he had second-class passage, Nordstrom slept with the mules.

Reaching Port Valdez, Alaska, in Prince William Sound, that summer was merely the beginning of Nordstrom's thousand-mile adventure to his ultimate destination: Dawson, the frontier town in the heart of the gold fields. He battled cold, snow, rain, storms, and wind—mostly on foot, because his horse died along the way and had to be butchered for food, which enabled him to survive.

From Skagway, he walked over the frozen solid Klondike River into tiny Dawson, only a year old, but "as lively a little place as you'd ever see," he recalled. "There were many saloons, dance halls, and gambling houses, all waiting for the poor miner to spend his hard-earned gold."

For the next two years, Nordstrom struggled in the gold fields, taking a series of jobs to keep going. Finally, his luck changed: He hit a gold strike. But another miner disputed Nordstrom's claim. That miner's brother was the local Land Commissioner, who was the final arbiter on disputed claims. John's friends advised him to make a settlement, rather than hold out for sole ownership and possibly end up with nothing. His share of the claim was worth $13,000 (about $300,000 in today's dollars), which "looked like a lot of money to me, so I decided that I had had enough of Alaska and returned to Seattle," he recalled.

A booming Seattle was roaring into the twentieth century, fueled by the financial windfall of an unprecedented rush of new arrivals and the Klondike Gold Rush. (The people who made the real money in the Gold Rush were the Seattle merchants who sold supplies to the aspiring miners.) "There was a swagger in its walk, a boldness in its vision," a historian wrote about Seattle. "Out here, on the edge of the continent, the great Pacific lapping at the front door, all things seemed possible."

Back in Seattle, John Nordstrom renewed his acquaintance with Hilda Carlson, a Swedish girl he had taken out a few times before going to Alaska. They married in 1900. John, who just turned 29, looked around for some small business to get into.

Carl F. Wallin, an old acquaintance from his Klondike days, had established a tiny shoe repair shop on Fourth Avenue and Pike Street in downtown Seattle. Nordstrom often visited Wallin at his shop, which consisted of a 10-foot-wide frontage. Eventually, Wallin suggested that the two men join in a partnership to open a shoe store. Nordstrom agreed. He put up $4,000 and Wallin $1,000. They were able to convince the real estate office occupying the next 10 feet to move out for $250. In 1901, they opened a 20-foot-wide shoe store, Wallin & Nordstrom.

In his 1950 memoir, Nordstrom recalled the very first day of business: "I had never fitted a pair of shoes or sold anything in my life, but I was depending on Mr. Wallin's meager knowledge of shoe salesmanship to help me out.

"Well, this opening day we had not had a customer by noon, so my partner went to lunch. He had not been gone but a few minutes when our first customer, a woman, came in for a pair of shoes she had seen in the window. I was nervous and could not find the style she had picked out in our stock.

"I was just about ready to give up when I decided to try on the pair from the window, the only pair we had of that style. I'll never know if it was the right size, but the customer bought them anyway."

Opening day sales totaled $12.50.

What is important about the story of Wallin & Nordstrom's first sale is that John Nordstrom, without even realizing it, hit on one of the foundations of the Nordstrom Way that continues to this day: *Do not let a woman leave the store without selling her a pair of shoes.*

Besides that, he established a culture whose cornerstone is: "Do whatever it takes to take care of the customer." More than 110 years later, the same principle applies.

Wallin & Nordstrom steadily grew their business, periodically moving to larger spaces in downtown Seattle. It was a business built on customer service.

John Nordstrom had a simple philosophy: Offer the customer the best possible service, selection, quality, and value. A true entrepreneur, he was in the store every day listening to what the customers liked and disliked about quality, fit, style, and so on. When a customer said, "I want a red pump in size 7B," he'd write that down on a piece of paper, and put it into his suit pocket, to remind him of what to have in his store to satisfy his customers and keep them loyal.

Everett, Elmer, and Lloyd

Eventually, John's eldest sons, Everett W., born in 1903, and Elmer J., born a year later, began working in the store when each of them reached the age of 12, establishing a Nordstrom family tradition that has continued to this day across four generations.

In the late 1920s, after gaining experience working for other retailers, Everett and Elmer bought out their father (who loaned them the money) and Carl Wallin, and took ownership of the business, which comprised a couple of stores and employed about a dozen clerks. They soon changed the name of the store from Wallin & Nordstrom to Nordstrom's and later to Nordstrom.

The Great Depression almost put them out of business. The brothers had agreed that if their father's interests were jeopardized, they would close, liquidate the business, and pay him off.

"I remember one night after everybody left, we locked the door, turned out the lights and we sat in the store, with the lights coming in from the outside," recalled Elmer. "The time was come where we were just about ready to close up. We talked for several hours. We finally said, let's give it another month's try. The next month picked up and we were off to the races. But if it hadn't picked up, we would have closed up that month, and there wouldn't have been a Nordstrom."

Younger brother Lloyd, born in 1910, later joined Everett and Elmer.

"I have to confess that we were all a bit retiring and weren't particularly strong salesmen," Elmer wrote in *A Winning Team*. "In fact, others could sell rings around us."

Aware of their own selling limitations, they hired men (only men at that time), who could move the product. In so doing, they established a culture where outstanding employees would be rewarded for achieving sales goals.

The brothers made sure they would not be undersold. They told customers that if they could find the same item for a lower price, they would gladly match that price. Today, a customer who finds the same item at a lower price can call or e-mail a Nordstrom salesperson, who will do a price match and refund or credit the difference.

As the company grew more prosperous, the brothers were legally required to have a more formal corporate structure. Everett, as the eldest, was the logical choice to be president. He agreed, but only if the three brothers rotated job titles—president, vice president, and secretary/treasurer—every two years.

"Occasionally people would ask us our titles and we sometimes had trouble remembering who was who on that day," wrote Elmer. "We had to know when signing papers, but that's the only time the members of the team needed a title."

Today, three brothers again lead Nordstrom. The company has no CEO. Blake, the oldest brother, is President; Peter, two years younger, is President of Merchandise, and Erik, two years younger than Peter, is President of Stores. They work as a team, just as their grandfather, Everett, did with his brothers in the second generation, and as their father, Bruce, did with the other members of the third generation.

Everett, the eldest brother, was a perfectionist about product quality. Once, an order of women's pumps was found to be poorly constructed.

The uppers were separating from the soles near the ball of the foot. When Everett alerted the manufacturer, he was told, "They're not all bad. Just send back the ones that come apart." Everett's reaction was to go into the stockroom, take every pair of shoes from that manufacturer and start popping them apart. Now they were all bad.

"He could do it easily with his thumb and he popped them by the hour, just to make sure that no customer would have a problem," wrote Elmer about his older brother.

Ensuring highest product quality is essential to the Nordstrom culture. This insistence on quality continues today with Everett's grandchildren—Blake, Peter, and Erik. In an industrial/retail area south of Seattle is the Nordstrom Quality Center, which is dedicated to making sure that the products the company sells will be of the highest quality and workmanship.

From all over the company-wide system, the facility receives defective shoes and clothing that can be repaired. Quality Center employees sort all of an individual vendor's merchandise into one bin, then invite the vendor's representative (or, in some cases, the principal of the company) to the facility to show them what common quality issues Nordstrom is facing with their merchandise, such as buttons that are poorly sewn on. Nordstrom offers feedback on how construction problems could be solved. Vendors who want to continue to sell to Nordstrom are grateful for the feedback.

The Quality Center has also helped Nordstrom to solve one of its historically major concerns ever since its strictly shoe store days: matching up the shoes that had lost their mates. That task was virtually impossible to do in individual stores, because, in the natural course of business, some shoes bought for one store might get transferred or returned to another store within the company.

Nordstrom used to put on "singles parties," where managers would spend one entire day in the distribution center matching up shoes. It was a waste of management's time and the problem got bigger as the company expanded in size and geographic reach. Today, the Quality Center refurbishes and shines up mismated shoes as well as shoes that were worn and returned by customers. The spruced-up shoes are marked down and then sent to Rack stores.

Typical of Nordstrom, most of the workers at the Quality Center are veteran employees who have worked on the sales floor, so they are familiar with merchandise construction and know what to look for.

Third Generation: Bruce, John, Jim, and Jack

Everett, Elmer, and Lloyd built Nordstrom into the biggest independent shoe retailer in the United States. After World War II, they began to expand, along with the rest of peacetime America. In 1950, they opened their first out-of-town store in Portland, Oregon, and then their first shopping center store at Northgate Mall in Seattle. They would gradually grow to have eight shoe stores in Washington State and Oregon. Taking advantage of other opportunities, they operated leased shoe departments in 13 department stores in the western United States and Hawaii. Under that arrangement, Nordstrom ran the shoe departments independent of the rest of the department store. They paid rent and gave back a percentage of sales to the department stores.

Solely a shoe store since its founding, Nordstrom expanded into women's apparel in 1963 with the acquisition of a Seattle specialty shop called Best's Apparel, a fashionable downtown Seattle retailer with a second store in downtown Portland, and the brothers renamed the company "Nordstrom Best."

The Nordstroms believed that if you can be successful selling shoes, then you can apply those same principles to other merchandise departments. But their entry into apparel was initially greeted with skepticism by manufacturers who "weren't very enthused to see us on buying trips," recalled Elmer, "but that only reminded us of our early days in shoes.

It was like starting over in many ways, and that was exciting. No one really believed that shoe store owners could be successful with apparel. No one, except us."

The apparel industry's reservations about Nordstrom continued for almost a decade. Cynthia Paur, who eventually became a high-ranking Nordstrom merchandise manager, said that when she first became a buyer in the 1970s (when Nordstrom had only five full-line stores), "we had a difficult time securing a lot of the hot lines that we wanted to buy. We were the little guys."

One of the reasons Nordstrom moved into apparel was to offer more opportunities for the third generation of Nordstroms, then in their thirties, including Everett's son, Bruce A.; Elmer's two sons, James F. and John N.; and John "Jack" McMillan, who was married to Lloyd's daughter, Loyal. All four were University of Washington graduates with degrees in business, just like their fathers.

Like their fathers, the three younger Nordstroms began working in the store as children and continued to sell shoes throughout high school and college; McMillan also started working for the store while an undergraduate.

Trained on the sales floor, the third generation was literally and figuratively "raised kneeling in front of the customer," said Bruce. Actually, they toiled for years in the stockroom before their fathers "ever allowed us near a foot."

In 1968, the brothers, whose net worth and only source of income was the corporation, wanted their estates to have a market value that could be readily established for the purpose of estate taxes. Their alternatives were to either sell the chain to the next generation or to an established retailer.

Because the younger Nordstroms lacked the capital, the first option was not viable. However, the second option was not only viable, it was preferable because it would make the brothers wealthy. Everett, Elmer, and Lloyd notified the third generation that they intended to sell the company, and soon three of the most prominent department store chains of that era—Associated Dry Goods, Dayton-Hudson, and Broadway-Hale Stores (the company later known as Carter Hawley Hale)—emerged as the prominent suitors.

But the younger Nordstroms didn't want to work for one of those three retail giants—and didn't think they'd last very long.

They presented a detailed business plan to their fathers, whom they needed to convince that they could do a better job of running the company than any outside organization. The plan included paying for the transaction by issuing stock and taking the company public.

"We asked them to entrust their fortune to us," said Bruce.

The brothers of the second generation believed the main reason they had succeeded was their ability to work together as a cohesive unit. They didn't know whether the third generation, who had always gotten along (but had not had the opportunity to work as a group) could duplicate that solidarity. "And we didn't want to see them break up into feuding factions trying to," recalled Elmer.

The younger generation was shocked when the brothers accepted their offers.

Ed Carter, chairman of Broadway-Hale Stores, flew to Seattle to try to have the decision reversed. He told the third generation of Nordstroms that they would be the biggest shareholders in the department store chain—which they would be running. That didn't interest them. They wanted to do their own thing with their own family store.

The pro forma proposal put together by the third generation estimated that Nordstrom would reach $100 million in sales by 1980. As it turned out, they underestimated that number by almost $400 million.

In May 1970, Bruce, then 37; John N., 34; James, 31; and Jack McMillan, 39, assumed operating management. The following year, the three Nordstroms became copresidents and directors, and drew the same salary. They were following the same power-sharing formula by which Nordstrom is still run today. Elmer, Everett, and

Lloyd became cochairmen of the board, "offering encouragement and resisting the temptation to give advice," wrote Elmer. As the torch was passed, the older brothers emphasized the need for constant diligence, "Because from our experience during the war years, we saw how easily a business could fall apart from neglect." They gave the younger generation a long list of potential excuses—including the weather, the economy, and the new shopping center down the block. "We told them they might as well give us their excuses by the number, because they didn't mean a thing. If business was bad, there was nowhere to put the blame but upon themselves."

Like their predecessors, the third generation emulated the decision-by-consensus approach, and it worked; whatever private disagreements they had were never known by anyone outside their inner circle.

They also remained committed to doing whatever was necessary to take care of the customers. For example, a man once wrote a letter describing his difficulty in getting a suit to fit that he had purchased at Nordstrom, despite several visits for alterations. When John N. got the letter, he sent over a new suit to the customer's office, along with a Nordstrom tailor to make sure the jacket and pants were perfect. When alterations were completed, the suit was delivered at no charge.

Betting Everything on Southern California

In the 1970s, Nordstrom, which some were calling the "Bloomingdale's of the West," was asked to open a store in what was to become one of the greatest shopping centers in the world: South Coast Plaza in Costa Mesa, California.

It was a huge financial gamble because Nordstrom was not well known outside of the Pacific Northwest. A failure could have sunk the company.

In May 1978, Nordstrom opened a 127,000-square-foot, three-level store at South Coast Plaza. This store boasted the biggest shoe department in the state of California—10,000 square feet for women's shoes, 3,000 for men's, and 2,500 for children's. Although the Nordstrom name was barely known, the store became an instant success and quickly grew to be the biggest volume store in the chain.

The third generation grew the company to 61 full-line stores in Washington, Alaska, Oregon, California, Utah, Texas, Minnesota, Indiana, Illinois, Pennsylvania, Virginia, Maryland, New Jersey, and New York; 20 clearance and off-price stores; a Faconnable men's wear boutique in New York City; and leased shoe departments in 12 department stores in Hawaii and Guam—with total sales of $4.1 billion and a reputation as America's number-one customer service company.

And by the way, Carter Hawley Hale went out of business in 1991.

A Crisis of Confidence

Nordstrom is not the perfect company. The perfect company has yet to be invented. In fact, in the late 1990s, Nordstrom went through a rough patch that threatened the future of the Nordstrom way.

In 1995, Bruce, John, Jim, and Jack (the third generation) decided to step down as cochairmen. They continued serving on the board of directors and as members of the board's executive committee, but they tried a power-sharing approach with four (later two) key executives who were not members of the Nordstrom family. It was a failed experiment. Business was up and down. Service was not as consistent as it used to be. Nordstrom's reputation was bruised. The opinion of the media was summed up in a March 24, 1997 *Time* magazine double-page article that was headlined "Losing Its Luster." A color photograph of a crushed Nordstrom gift box, wrapped in tattered ribbon, accompanied it. During this period, Nordstrom suffered through what might be called a crisis of confidence. The company spent multimillions of dollars on consultants in a desperate effort to figure out how to get its groove back.

In the fall of 2000, the Nordstrom board decided to bring in new leadership to replace John Whitacre, the only non-Nordstrom family member in 99 years to be chief executive officer, a job he had held since 1997.

On the face of it, Whitacre should have been able to carry on the tradition. Whitacre, then 47, had been with the company ever since his student days at the University of Washington, when he starting selling shoes, and then he had worked up the ladder of the organization.

He set out to modernize the accounting, merchandising, and buying systems, and to solve the company's chronic problem of overstocked inventory. He was in a difficult position, between the third and the fourth generations of Nordstroms. He oversaw the elimination of several women's apparel departments, a reorganization of the selection, and an increase in the assortment of high-fashion items. But, in the process, he shifted the company's traditional primary focus from the customers and the salespeople to the shareholders. That may sound odd to investors, but not to longtime followers of Nordstrom.

Although several well-known outside retail executives were interested in taking over the helm, the board selected Blake Nordstrom, then 39 and president of the company's Nordstrom Rack clearance store division, to become president of the company. His father, Bruce, then 66, agreed to return as chairman, a position he had shared with his two cousins and a cousin-in-law until they all stepped down in 1995.

Blake became the first fourth-generation Nordstrom to lead the company. His brother Peter eventually became President of Merchandise and youngest brother Erik became the President of Stores. Like their grandfather, father, uncles, and cousins, Blake and his brothers Peter and Erik began working in the store as young boys, sweeping the floors and stocking merchandise at age 13. They worked their way up from selling shoes on the floor to attaining executive positions.

At that time, Nordstrom had 114 stores in 23 states and annual sales of more than $5 billion.

Although some analysts were disappointed by the selection of Blake, the choice was generally cheered by Nordstrom insiders, from frontline salespeople to longtime managers—not as a knock against Whitacre, who was universally liked, but as a signal that the Nordstrom family was back in charge.

The elevation of Blake and the return of Bruce were akin to Steve Jobs reassuming the helm at Apple Computer—it was that profound, and the potential resurgence turned out to be just as dramatic.

At a time when there are few superstar retailing CEOs, it would have been a mistake to recruit an outsider who could not appreciate—or lead—the culture.

At a press conference after his selection, Blake declared that Nordstrom's business "is all about the customer. What works best for us is taking care of our customers and listening to them one at a time."

One disappointed analyst dismissed that comment: "I don't see [Blake's promotion] as much of a change," he said. "They talked about customer service and about listening to customers, the same platitudes we have heard before."

But at Nordstrom, customer service is not a cliché or a strategy; it's the core of the company's culture. In fact, a primary reason that Blake became president was to reaffirm that culture, which he embodied.

As an example, consider this story: A few years ago, Blake scheduled a lunch with Jim Donald, then the Chief Executive Office of another famous Seattle company: Starbucks. Donald asked Blake if he wouldn't mind stopping by the tailor shop of the downtown flagship store on his way to the lunch, and bringing with him two pair of slacks that Donald had had altered.

"Blake said, 'Sure, no problem,'" Donald remembered. "We had lunch. We both forgot about the pants. That evening at nine o'clock, there's a knock at my door. There's Blake with those two pairs of pants. I said, 'Man, that's what I call service.'"

Why is it important to have a Nordstrom family member in charge?

"There's something magical about how the Nordstroms feel toward the customer that just connects with employees," said a retired company executive. "The passion of the Nordstrom family for this business is hard to replicate." He cited how meaningful it is for frontline people to have a Nordstrom walk into their store and ask them what they need to do their job better. "The people on the sales floor think: If these Nordstroms are fighting it out, I'm going to fight it out, too."

That's exactly what the Nordstroms did. Over the next six weeks after taking over, Bruce, Blake, Peter, and Erik traveled around the country, speaking with top salespeople, soliciting their opinions on what went wrong and how things could be fixed. They were told that the company seemed to have lost confidence in its sales leaders' ability to inform management of problems on the front lines. Salespeople "felt maybe we didn't trust them anymore and we weren't listening to them, that we didn't value them as much," said Blake, who added that the old policy was "bottom-up management—where managers were there to facilitate sales staff. But the company now had bosses who said 'I am the manager and I know all the answers.'"

Bruce wrote in his memoir, *Leave It Better Than You Found It*, that those encounters with employees were "a tempering experience. We asked for criticism and we got it, but it was positive criticism from loyal employees. At the end, I felt strangely invigorated. These are amazing folks. They were a little ticked off and certainly had things to say. I felt so good about the amount of input I got. Listening to our people helped this company more than anything else we could have done. Ask your top people what they need, because they have the answers."

By going back to the basics, Nordstrom turned things around. On August 19, 2004, a headline in the *Wall Street Journal* announced "Nordstrom Regains Its Luster." It has not lost its luster since.

While tradition and continuity of leadership are important, the Nordstrom family is not insulated from non-Nordstrom thinking. Today, the majority of the board of directors is comprised of outside businessmen and businesswomen, and the upper management team is a mix of nonfamily and family members.

Clearly, the continuity of family management is one of the most important reasons for Nordstrom's success. The active presence and involvement of family members is the guarantee that Nordstrom will remain Nordstrom; without them, it would be a different company. The Nordstroms have been involved and instrumental in every aspect of the company. At store openings, the family meets with every new hire. The arrival of these three tall, blond Swedes, often accompanied by their cousin, Jamie, President of Nordstrom Direct, is an exciting time for employees.

"It's so powerful when they come around to talk to our people and remind them that our company is only as good as they are today and every day," said an executive vice president and regional manager.

Sales Are the Truth

Nordstrom withstood the Great Recession better than all of its rivals. Despite its position in the hard-hit luxury retail sector, Nordstrom never experienced a quarterly loss during the economic downturn. When sales fell sharply, the company focused on getting its inventories and expenses aligned with projected sales.

Nordstrom's commitment to customers guided its expense management. The company questioned every aspect of its operations that did not enhance the shopping experience. The company focused on its long-term strategy of improving the quality of the customers' experience, both in stores and online. They wanted to protect the things that helped them take care of customers while scaling back other costs. This meant becoming leaner, primarily at the back of the house—the areas of the business that did not directly engage with customers. This editing and prioritizing based on the customer enabled Nordstrom to manage its business more effectively and profitably.

By 2010, same-store sales increased by 8.1 percent, helping to produce record sales of $9.31 billion. Nordstrom had its fastest-ever inventory turns—5.56 per year (the number of times that a company's inventory cycles), which is reflective of its ability to flow fresh product into stores.

Despite their success, the Nordstroms continue to insist on projecting a public image of disarming, small-town modesty that might strike an observer as disingenuous. They say that there is nothing special or magical or difficult about what they do and that the system is embarrassingly simple. "We outservice, not outsmart," is a typical Nordstromism. They rarely talk about themselves or draw attention to themselves. That would be very un-Nordstrom-like behavior. When Bruce was selected as *Footwear News* magazine's Man of the Year, he politely declined the award and refused to be interviewed for the article.

Jim's father, Elmer, wrote in his memoir, "Many people think that we Nordstroms are secretive because we don't talk much about ourselves. The truth is, we can't afford to boast. If we did, we might start to believe our own stories, get big heads, and stop trying.

"Our success is simply a matter of service, selection, fair pricing, hard work, and plain luck. As the owners, we felt that we should work harder than anyone else. If we didn't, our lackadaisical attitude would spread to the next level, and the next level on down until everyone was taking it easy."

"It's not about us," said Blake, who described his role and that of his family members as "stewards of the business and the culture. We are here to help everyone achieve his or her goals. Companies that have a strong culture have an asset—a point of difference. We try to create an atmosphere where people feel valued, trusted, respected, and empowered, where they have a proprietary feeling and an entrepreneurial spirit. The magic occurs when all these things come together."

A Seattle journalist once compared the Nordstrom family to stately Mount Rainier. "As the mountain symbolizes the beauty and splendor of the Northwest," wrote Fred Moody in *Seattle Weekly*, "so the Nordstrom name has come to epitomize a certain Northwestness of character, a set of drives and values that we regard as being unique to our corner of the country."

2

Hire With Care

Finding the Right Fit for the Culture

In our system, employees must have a competitive spirit because we start comparing them the day they walk in the door. That's one of the best ways we know how to improve. If we have competitive people, we can accomplish something.

—James F. Nordstrom (1940–1996)

Nordstrom is not just another department store. Many people think of a department store as a place where you hang out for a while before you get a real job. At most other department stores, employees are *clerks*—powerless functionaries, who slavishly follow the rules, don't make waves, and don't give very good service. At Nordstrom, the worst thing you can say about a salesperson is that he or she is just "clerking" it.

Nordstrom is looking to hire *entrepreneurs*—empowered self-starters, who seize opportunities to create and build their own businesses; to be franchisees within the larger Nordstrom franchise.

Nordstrom management is keenly aware that every employee will eventually have an impact on the customer experience—whether on the front lines or in a support position. Consequently, because the company empowers employees to treat the business as if it were their own, it looks for entrepreneurs who create excitement and passion around their business, and who can also build strong relationships, both with the customer and with other team members throughout the entire company.

In the words of Niccolo Machiavelli, the Italian author and historian of the fifteenth century, "Entrepreneurs are simply those who understand that there is little difference between obstacle and opportunity and are able to turn both to their advantage."

Welcome to Nordstrom

Arriving at the lobby of the Nordstrom corporate offices, which is connected to the flagship store in downtown Seattle, a visitor is greeted first by the Nordstrom history and culture. On the walls adjacent to the elevators is a grainy, early-twentieth-century picture of founder John W. Nordstrom and his original partner, Carl F. Wallin, proudly standing outside their first tiny shoe store. There is another shot, circa 1910, of the interior of that store, where mustachioed salesmen in rumpled suits are dwarfed by stacks and stacks of shoe boxes that are collected along the walls and piled high up to the ceiling.

New Seattle-area employees now attend orientation on the fifth floor of this building, which contains the John W. Nordstrom room, the venue for annual shareholders' meetings, special customer events, staff meetings, and pep rallies. All around are pictures of stores, of various generations of Nordstroms, and numerous other reminders of the rich Nordstrom heritage and its identifiable and sustainable culture.

An appreciation of what Nordstrom is all about cannot be fully grasped without an understanding of the company's culture. That is why the importance and the value of the culture are emphasized from the moment potential new employees interview to work for the company.

On one particular day, a dozen well-groomed and neatly dressed men and women are seated behind a horseshoe configuration of gray tables in the fifth-floor meeting room. They are a racially diverse group; most are under the age of 30, a couple are closer to 50. What they have in common is that they are all new employees awaiting the start of employee orientation, which kicks off their career at Nordstrom. They have come here for several reasons: an opportunity for personal and professional growth; freedom to be entrepreneurial and successful; to be a part of something meaningful; and to feel valued.

In front of each one of them is a half-inch-thick blue folder. The one word on the cover is "Welcome."

On the inside, a separate sheet of paper contains these words:

As we travel along the road of life, we encounter paths that lead to a great opportunity for growth. To recognize the doors that open to a bright future is the key. Once inside, we crave support from our colleagues. We know that the health of our relationships is paramount to our own success, and that the joy of sharing ideas leads to a diversity of options. Our reward is access to a wealth of knowledge that we would have otherwise overlooked. Welcome to Nordstrom. Our door is open.

Inside the packet are separate folders containing information on the company, employee guidelines, compensation program, safety program, and employee benefits. There is also a 5½-inch by 7½-inch card—the Nordstrom Employee Handbook (See Figure 2.1). One side of the card says:

Welcome to Nordstrom. We're glad you're here! Our number one goal is to provide outstanding customer service. Set both your personal and professional goals high. We have great confidence in your ability to achieve them, so our employee handbook is very simple. We have only one rule:

Flipping the card over reveals the one rule: *Use good judgment in all situations.*

That's it. This single directive is the foundation upon which the Nordstrom Way is built.

Use good judgment in all situations. (We discuss this in more depth in Chapter 4: Empower Entrepreneurs to Own the Customer Experience.)

For some of these men and women, this day marks the birth of a long-term relationship that will bring them financial rewards and professional

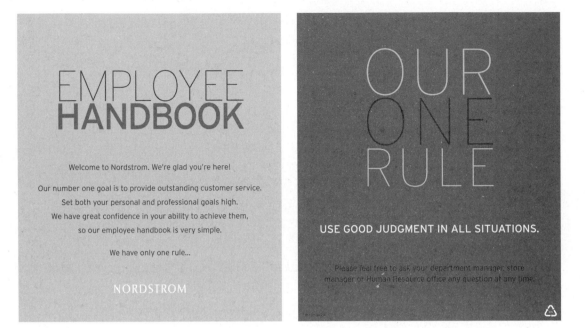

Figure 2.1   Nordstrom Employee Handbook

and personal fulfillment. For others, it is the beginning of the end. They will eventually leave Nordstrom because of what they will perceive as unreasonable demands, persistent pressure to reach a ceaseless series of sales goals, and relentless emphasis on providing the kind of all-encompassing customer service that has fed the Nordstrom mystique. But the future is for later. On this orientation day, these men and women are here to immerse themselves in that culture and its history.

The people attending orientation, like all other Nordstrom employees, will become steeped in the culture. They will learn the values that the company supports and the atmosphere it tries to create, where everyone is in a position to succeed. All of that comes from the top and works its way through every part of the organization.

During this early period, Nordstrom wants new employees to instantaneously connect with the company as a whole and with their home store in particular, to help them understand what is special about their team, and to get them excited about their new careers. They are schooled in the Nordstrom service philosophy and encouraged to work on enhancing the customer service experience one customer at a time. They learn about the company's history, culture, and experience by watching video interviews with members of the Nordstrom family and top-performing employees. In person, they hear from successful store managers, department managers, and salespeople, who share their own history with the company and their advice on how to achieve great things.

Nordstrom consistently reinforces the message that every single decision the company makes is for the benefit of customers and that these employees are crucial to that process.

They will later watch many other videos, including "Seeing Your Business Through the Eyes of the Customer," as well as "A Day in the Life of Buyers" on a New York buying trip, and how they can benefit from profit sharing and their 401(k) plan.

They are learning every aspect of the company and how each aspect works and fits in with the overall culture.

Values and Practices

Nordstrom's leaders explain the difference between the company's values and its practices.

"Values define who we are, and if they change we will become something else," Peter Nordstrom wrote in the employee publication, *Loop*. He described practices as "ways of doing things" and "behaviors that express our values. Practices may serve us well for long periods of time—but they are not values, and therefore can be changed without changing our culture. Practices are all the things that deliver these values; they change and evole over time." Nordstrom executives are constantly asking themselves what parts of the culture should never change and what parts must change in order to maintain their core values. These core values include:

- Creating a customer-first service mentality.
- Producing an honest and ethical way of doing business.
- Delivering compelling value.
- Treating people with respect.
- Rewarding hard work and results.
- Choosing to err on the customer's behalf.

James Collins, author of the seminal business book, *Built to Last* (which spotlights Nordstrom) wrote, "People always ask me, how do you teach core values? The answer is, you don't. The goal is not to get people to share your core values. It's to get people who already share your core values."

Nordstrom shares this belief.

Hire Motivated People—Who Are Also Nice

In the 1920s and 1930s, when they began to expand their business, John W. Nordstrom's three sons—Everett, Elmer, and Lloyd—created a sales-driven entrepreneurial culture by recruiting "fiery producers, tough guys, men who had to work hard to put bread on the table," Elmer once said. Hiring these self-described "shoe dogs," who were attracted to the Nordstrom system where employees earned commissions on each and every shoe sale, "was usually a shot in the dark. In most cases, we just looked them over, gave them a shoehorn, and watched how they performed."

Even though Elmer (the last surviving second-generation Nordstrom, who died in 1993 at the age of 89) was describing the Nordstrom philosophy of more than eight decades ago, that philosophy still holds true today. A can-do attitude, a positive personality, and a strong work ethic are still the primary ingredients for success at Nordstrom. Some things will never change.

The qualities that Nordstrom looks for in its employees couldn't be more basic. First of all, the company wants its salespeople to be nice.

"We can hire nice people and teach them to sell," chairman emeritus Bruce Nordstrom likes to say, "but we can't hire salespeople and teach them to be nice."

The Nordstrom corollary to that philosophy is *hire the smile, train the skill*.

"We are often asked how we find people who want to give our level of customer service," said Bruce. "Most of the time, they find us. Some people might think our way of doing things is too gung ho for them. Okay, then don't work here. This is not a job for clock-watchers."

Nordstrom provides little in the way of a formalized training program. When asked who trains his salespeople, Bruce's simple answer was "their parents." Or their grandparents or guardians—whoever raised them and instilled them with a set of values.

What company or organization doesn't want to hire nice, motivated people? Of course, they all do. The difference is that Nordstrom and other great customer service companies want to hire people who are *already* nice and *already* motivated to do a good job before they walk through the door to apply for a job.

Have you ever tried to take someone who is not inherently nice and magically make them nice? It can't be done. Isn't it amazing how many times during the course of our day we cross paths with people who deal with the public, but are not nice? These people, who are the public voice or public face of a company or an organization, often give the impression that they just don't like people. You want to shake them by the shoulders and yell, "Find another line of work! Become a lighthouse keeper, but don't work in a job where you have to deal with people!"

Nordstrom believes the key to good customer service is to hire good people and keep working with them, nurturing them, and giving them the tools that they need to succeed. Those tools include attractive, inviting stores; high-quality merchandise; a wide range of product choices and sizes; and customer-friendly policies such as the Nordstrom return policy, which is virtually unconditional, no questions asked.

Previous retail experience has never been a prerequisite. In fact, if a job applicant has already worked in retail, that might be a detriment because the applicant may have developed bad customer service habits, such as reflexively saying "no" to the customer rather than "yes."

Nordstrom recruits at colleges and job fairs and offers internship programs for aspiring Nordies. Many Nordstrom recruiters originally started out on the sales floor, so they know what they are looking for in potential candidates. Salespeople come from all walks of life. But they bring with themselves a strong desire to give great customer service.

A college degree has never been a requirement. Enthusiasm, a desire to work hard, and a capacity to generate your own traffic are much more important in a system that can best be described as a process of natural selection—a purely Darwinian survival of the fittest.

Once a candidate has applied, he or she goes through a phone screen with a recruiter or a person in Human Resources, followed by in-person interviews with a department manager and a store manager. Although candidates meet with assorted members of the store team, the hiring decision ultimately lies with the department manager. Nordstrom provides managers with a variety of training tools to help them make the best hiring decisions.

These new employees must buy into the culture and understand their role in maintaining and supporting the culture through their actions.

"Selling clothes isn't what we do," said a retired Nordstrom executive. "It's filling people's needs and making them feel better emotionally."

Each honest, ethical, hardworking, and empathetic employee contributes to maintaining the customer service culture. Each employee must be a team player because it is through teamwork that the culture is formed and sustained.

New employees are put out on the sales floor and expected to grasp the values and expectations of the culture. They either catch it or they don't. They have to prove to management (and to themselves) that they believe in helping others and that they like to give good customer service. They must have a thorough knowledge of the products and services because it is through those products and services that relationships with customers are created, nurtured, and maintained.

Some people who work at Nordstrom may find that they are in the wrong job. If sales aren't for you, but you like the company, Nordstrom will find a place for you as a support person. They don't want to lose people who have been with the company for several years, because such people understand the culture and can be valuable team players.

Bob Love

A list of the kind of people who succeed at Nordstrom wouldn't be complete without a mention of Bob Love.

Back in the 1970s, Love was one of the top players in the National Basketball Association. He played 11 seasons, most of them with the Chicago Bulls, and was the team's leading scorer for seven straight years. Before Michael Jordan came along, Love held all of the Bulls' scoring records, and was a three-time NBA All-Star. Unfortunately, Love had a severe stutter, which had kept him from being able to endorse products or be interviewed by the media. Toward the end of his career, he was traded to the Seattle SuperSonics. After hurting his back, Love was forced to retire. He went through much adversity, losing his money, his wife, and much of his self-respect. In the early 1980s, after seven years of trying to find a steady job, he found himself busing tables and washing dishes at the restaurant in the Nordstrom flagship store in downtown Seattle, where he was paid $4.45 an hour.

It was hard to miss this 6′8″ black man cleaning tables. Love could overhear the whispers: "Hey, that's Bob Love. He used to be a great basketball player. What a shame."

After working for a year and a half at Nordstrom, Love was taken aside by cochairman John N. Nordstrom of the third generation, who praised Love's work and, more importantly, told him that the only way he was going to advance in the company was if he could find a way to deal with his speech impediment. John N. offered to help pay for Love's speech training. Eventually, for the first time in his life, Love could speak without stuttering. He ultimately rose up through the ranks to become a diversity affairs manager for Nordstrom, until he was hired by the Chicago Bulls to become director of community affairs. Even more impressive is the fact that, today, Bob Love is a highly sought-after inspirational and motivational speaker.

It's Not a Job for Everyone

For many years, Betsy Sanders was vice president and general manager for Nordstrom's Southern California division. As a retail industry leader, she frequently met with her regional competitors for United Way meetings and the like, and on those occasions, she would invariably be taken aside by one of her competitors who wanted to know, confidentially, where Nordstrom found all those gung ho salespeople who enjoyed working in a hotly competitive system.

"Those retailers never got it," recalled Sanders, now a retail consultant and a former longtime member of the board of directors of Walmart Stores, Inc. "We got our people from the same employee pool they did. The difference between Nordstrom and its competitors was that the Nordstroms didn't go around talking about how wretched their people were. The Nordstroms thought they had great people. And look at the result.

"People would ask me if it was true that if you don't do a good job at Nordstrom you're gone. I'd say, 'Yes, I hope so.'"

Nordstrom is about selling. You don't get to rack up more than $9 billion in annual sales by just smiling and being nice.

Reminders of selling are constant. Signs are posted in employee areas (hallways, elevators, stockrooms, etc.) that ensure that everyone understands the same philosophy of service and selling. There is a "How Much Can You Sell?" bulletin board with advice on how to improve one's results.

Every top salesperson in each store is recognized by performance rankings that reflect the previous day's sales, the number of newly opened credit accounts, or how the store performed on a company-wide initiative. The company is constantly benchmarking, recognizing exceptional results, and sharing useful information to help employees produce. Bulletin boards have photos of top performers, laudatory customer service letters, and stories of legendary customer service.

There are also inspirational signs, such as:

"Through these doors pass the world's most courteous people."
"Nordstrom hires the very best people. That is why we hired you."
"Our customer service ethic is what built this company's reputation. Without that, we would be just another store."

Van Mensah, who sells men's suits in the suburban Washington, DC, Pentagon City (Virginia) store, is often asked to speak to new employees at Nordstrom. One of the top-performing salespeople in the chain for almost two decades, Van doesn't sugarcoat the demands of the job.

"Demands and expectations are high, but if you like working in an unrestricted environment, it's a great place to work," he explained. "Nordstrom provides you with great merchandise and the freedom to do what you want. I always tell people that if you're interested in retail, this is the best place to work. But you have to understand that this is not for everybody. It's a tough job, but if you have the discipline and you are willing to work hard and take the initiative, it's not that tough. After a while, it becomes easy, because you get used to so many things. It becomes a habit. With the tools and the resources the company provides, there's no reason for anybody not to make it."

Inverted Pyramid

Nordstrom's empowerment culture is illustrated by the company's informal structure of an inverted pyramid (see Figure 2.2). Customers sit atop the pyramid. Beneath them are the salespeople, department managers, and executives, all the way down to the board of directors. This is both a literal and symbolic way of how the company does

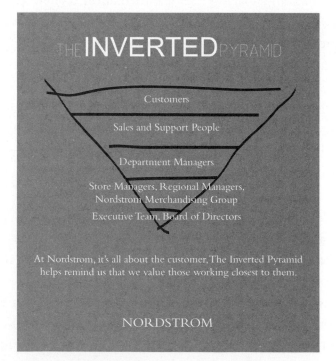

Figure 2.2 Inverted Pyramid

its business. The customers are obviously on top because they are the most important people in the equation. But the next most important are the salespeople because they are the ones who are closest to the customers. And it is the job of the rest of the workforce to help those people on the sales floor—the front lines—because they are the engines that power the machine. If they aren't making money, then the company isn't making money.

As a reminder that this is the case, the signature on employees' paychecks reads: "Blake Nordstrom on behalf of the customer."

The people at the top of the pyramid are constantly being supported by those below them. In fact, as employees rise up through the managerial and buying ranks, they are referred to as "moving down the pyramid."

The inverted pyramid was born in the early 1970s, when Nordstrom made its initial public offering of stock. A stock analyst asked the company for its organizational chart. To his surprise, none existed. Somebody suggested that "we take a pyramid and flip it upside down," recalled John N. Nordstrom. What sets Nordstrom apart is that, from department manager to chairman, all tiers of the inverted pyramid work to support the sales staff, not the other way around.

"The only thing we have going for us is the way we take care of our customers," explained Ray Johnson, retired cochairman, "and the people who take care of the customers are on the floor."

Because front-line people come in closest contact with customers, they must be empowered to establish relationships with customers and to find ways to take care of them. They must be able to listen to the customer, understand his or her needs, and follow through to fulfill them. If a salesperson can't find an item that a customer has requested, Nordstrom insists that the salesperson gets back to that customer to engender trust and loyalty. Customers want to do business with a company—and an individual—they can trust.

As long as you make the customer happy, no one has a problem with you. If you make the customer unhappy, everybody has a problem with you.

Empowering Managers and Buyers _____

Managers and buyers, who began their careers on the sales floor, are the keepers of the flame of the Nordstrom culture.

Back in the mid-twentieth century, while making buying decisions at the New York wholesale shoe markets, Everett Nordstrom of the second generation encouraged young buyers to develop their own ideas and make their own decisions. Everett's brother Elmer used to tell the story of what happened when one shoe manufacturer's sales staff showed their line to both Everett and a young buyer of women's shoes (the store's biggest department), and then turned to Everett for his reaction. "Don't talk to me," said Everett, "this is my buyer." The sales representatives then turned their eyes toward the nervous 22-year-old buyer. "After that, the fellow worked his heart out for the company," Elmer recalled.

Virtually all employees—including people who happen to have the last name Nordstrom—begin their careers on the selling floor, before they rise up through the ranks to become managers. Nordstrom employees universally appreciate the company's promote-from-within policy because it creates a culture where every manager and every buyer has gone through the same experiences as the people he or she is managing. No one manages until he or she has "walked in the shoes" of those being managed.

Clear evidence of this culture of upward mobility is that only a small handful of corporate officers (in specialized roles) came from outside the company; all of the others rose from the stockroom and the selling floor.

You start at the bottom and do it the Nordstrom way, and those standards are nonnegotiable.

President Blake Nordstrom—like his brothers, Peter and Erik—first began working in the store at the age of 12, sweeping floors in the downtown shoe stockroom. At 13, he stocked shoes; at 15, he began selling shoes. Later, he worked on the sales floor while attending the University of Washington, and after graduation as a buyer, merchandiser, department manager, and store manager in Nordstrom stores around the country.

"Because we have a promote-from-within culture, in this company you don't graduate from college and go to the corner office," said Erik, president of full-line stores. While growing up, "the vast majority of my cousins worked at the store at one point or another. It was a very natural thing to come to the store after school to sell shoes or work at some similar level. Some of my cousins eventually decided to do other things. For me, I stuck with it because I liked it."

Erik felt it was a natural progression for him and his brothers to start working in stock and then moving "to co-third assistant in women's shoes, then to a second assistant," and so on long before ever taking on any management responsibilities. "We were all well served by that."

Peter, president of merchandise, "can't imagine doing my job, or any job I've ever had in this company, without being grounded in how it all plays out at the point of sale. For example, I would be of no help to a salesperson who has a question about returning a suit if I hadn't done that exact same thing a few times myself. The moment of truth is what happens between salespeople and customers. So every decision we make—based on every experience we have had—must go back to supporting the relationship between the salespeople and the customers."

Alfred E. Osborne, Jr., a retired Nordstrom director and Senior Associate Dean of UCLA's Anderson School of Management, said "Starting on the sales floor sends the signal from management that it values that role more than almost anything. All up and down the organization, people appreciate the importance of this function and what it means for everything else in the organization. It's critical."

The Nordstrom family's own sales experiences fostered an appreciation for what salespeople go through and what it takes to satisfy customers. As they readily conceded, when they were young salespeople and didn't have what the customer asked for, they weren't good enough salespeople to be able to switch the customer to another item.

Managers' Responsibilities

Managers create, maintain, and support the corporate service culture. Therefore, they must have an appreciation and awareness of the company's history, culture, guiding principles, trials and tribulations, failures and successes.

Senior managers' responsibilities include hiring the right people, then empowering, managing, mentoring, praising, rewarding, and retaining those people. They create the atmosphere and the culture, but it is up to the people on the front lines to do the rest.

Because they have experienced every level of the organization, front-line managers know what to look for in a new hire, and they know how to empower those people, mentor them, recognize them, and praise them for a job well done.

Rather than sit behind a desk, managers are expected to spend some of their time on the selling floor (like the proprietors of small boutiques) interacting with the customers and the sales staff. They are paid a salary plus commission on any sales they make, and are eligible for a bonus tied to percentage increases in sales over the previous year.

Some consider the role of department manager to be the most difficult in the company because of so much responsibility. But the managers are in the position to teach people and build strong teams.

The store manager's primary responsibility is to set the tone for what happens on the sales floor, interacting with the salespeople, and the customers.

"Much of what happens in this company is environmental," said a manager from the East Coast. "You absorb it by watching and seeing the focus and priorities, and it snowballs."

A Nordstrom store manager in the Pacific Northwest said that part of her job is to promote an attitude among store employees that reflects: "It's not 'this is my department and that's your department.' It's 'this is our store, our customer, our results.'"

When a longtime employee became manager of a women's apparel department at a West Coast store in Sacramento, California, she was faced with a department that had experienced a lot of turnover. "So my number-one goal was to make sure we had stability," she said. "Once you have stability and happy people, you can create ongoing customer relationships, and that's how your business grows."

To instill a sense of ownership in her team, she decided to divide the responsibilities in the department. She assigned each person an area of accountability, such as customer service, new accounts, and developing personal trade.

One salesperson took the responsibility for new accounts. She made a chart to monitor each employee's progress, encouraged her teammates, and awarded prizes to those who signed up the most new accounts. The team rose to number-one in new accounts for their Nordstrom store, even though they are one of the store's smallest departments.

Taking this approach, "made the department more fun, because each person knew he or she could make an impact," said the department manager. "We continually challenge each other every day to be better."

The teamwork boosted the department's spirit and, as a result, the department soon racked up the number-one sales-per-hour increase in the company.

Buyers' Responsibilities

A women's sportswear buyer for the company's Rack discount division, appreciated the fact that Nordstrom allows its buyers the freedom "to help create and shape a department and gives us the full authority to do what we need to do to make a business exist."

Nordstrom buyers have to be just as aware of customer service as salespeople. After they purchase the merchandise, buyers must "sell" it to their sales teams so that the teams can sell it to the customers.

Buyers are always trying new ways to merchandise and share ideas with salespeople around the country.

Communication with the sales staff is obviously an essential part of the buyer's job. Nordstrom's best buyers support the salespeople in the stores. The buyers work for the salespeople; the salespeople don't work for the buyers. That's what Nordstrom's Inverted Pyramid structure is all about.

"My customer service is to my managers and salespeople because they are talking to the customers," says a buyer. "I need their feedback to help shape my buy."

Buyers get their feedback directly from the salespeople and the customers because they are encouraged to spend several hours a week on the sales floor. Interacting with the customer is powerful. Computer spreadsheets can tell you what's selling, but they can't tell you what you're not selling because you don't have it in stock. The best buyers at Nordstrom are good listeners. Customers appreciate being able to talk directly with a manager or a buyer. If a customer wants to know when a particular shoe will be in stock, a salesperson can turn to his or her buyer or manager and get the answer immediately.

Feedback

Nordstrom has many ways to get feedback from the people on the sales floor. For example, every year, the company flies in to Seattle all the salespeople who have recorded a million dollars or more in sales.

"We are closest to the market," said Van Mensah, a million-dollar performer. "We talk about different trends; what we need to do to improve the business. A lot of things we talk about get implemented. We give that advice freely. The company saves a lot of money by getting advice from people inside the company rather than bringing in a consultant who has no clue on how to sell to a customer. Our markets are different. By bringing in all these people from different markets, you get a good idea of your total business."

Because salespeople are so close to the customer, their feedback is essential for upper management. For example, the company created a Salesperson Advisory Board to get insight from women's apparel salespeople on a new floor layout concept that was implemented in selected stores throughout the country. The board was chosen by store managers to come together and respond to questions about how the program was working and to provide their honest opinions on how the new floor design was working for the salesperson's particular store and customers.

At the Rack, Nordstrom's clearance store division, they send out informal surveys to employees, called "What Would You Do?" to get insight into topics such as improving service and "What two things can we improve upon in your department and/or store?"

Nader Shafii, a million-dollar salesman in the South Coast Plaza store in Orange County, California, recollected in particular a meeting where then-cochairman James Nordstrom (who died in 1996) addressed buyers and managers and some Pacesetters (top-performing salespeople).

"Mr. Jim told the buyers and managers that the salespeople on the floor were the most important people in the company because they are the people between management and the customers," recalled Shafii. "He said, 'The salespeople are the ones who can bring the message from the customers to management—they tell us what they need in order to be able to make the customers happy. If the salespeople are not happy with the product, the buyers and managers should know. You should be able to react to that.' To me, that was a huge statement. That was the turning point for me."

Like all top Nordstrom salespeople, Shafii feels that he is running his own business, with the support of every level of management.

"If you are willing to go above and beyond the call of duty, Nordstrom is 100 percent behind you," said Shafii. "You have all the support and all the tools. It's up to you to see where you would like to go with it."

Customer service at Nordstrom is not just about selling clothes and shoes. "We're selling service, too," said Pat McCarthy. "We can convince customers that we are here to serve them—not just to take their money—by making their experience at Nordstrom easy. Sometimes that means being the concierge. I used to get all kinds of requests that are not clothes-related. People asked me the name of a good hotel, or a nice place to have dinner, or where to get a massage. If I didn't have the answer, I'd find out right away. Gas stations don't sell only gas; sometimes they sell directions."

Using Experienced "Nordies" to Spread the Culture

Because Nordstrom considers its culture the key element separating it from the competition, when the company expands to other regions, it relies on experienced "Nordies" to transfer to these new markets, to bring the culture with them and to teach and inspire new employees to give customer service the Nordstrom way.

Betsy Sanders, a former Nordstrom executive who in the late 1970s was put in charge of Nordstrom's move to California (the company's first expansion outside of the Pacific Northwest), recalled that California was "fraught with challenge[s] but it was exciting. There was no matrix, no plan, no instruction, which had always been how Nordstrom worked. Except this was on a bigger scale than we normally did it. We invented this region as we went along."

One of Sanders's first orders of business was to recruit people to work in the store.

"No one had been hired with the exception of the shoe buyer. At first, we were told that we could not find anyone in Southern California to give the kind of service that we had developed a reputation for. And if we did, it wouldn't matter because we would find no customers interested in us. We were virtually unknown in Southern California. People would stand in the middle of the mall and look down toward our end and say, 'What's a Nordstein?' I heard that more than once. The only people who had heard of us were those who had lived in the Northwest, and they were crazy about the fact that we were coming."

To attract new employees, Nordstrom ran a clever newspaper advertisement with the headline, "Wanted: People Power," accompanied by copy that described the attributes that Nordstrom was looking for. "It didn't say what we were. It didn't say what jobs were available," said Sanders. "On the strength of that ad, we had over 1,500 applicants. The personnel manager, the customer service manager, customer credit manager, and myself interviewed all 1,500; again, many of them had never heard of Nordstrom, but they loved what the ad called for." In keeping with the Nordstrom policy of hiring from within, all the new buyers and department managers for the California store were company veterans.

"The customers liked us, but our competitors waited for us to send everybody back to Seattle," said Sanders. "They presumed we just brought in [customer service experts] for the opening and that it would then be back to business as usual. Well, it never turned into business as usual. Eventually, competitors began telling employees in their training classes that they were going to have to start smiling and being nice to the customer because Nordstrom was coming and that's how Nordstrom salespeople act. They never got the point: It wasn't an act."

A decade later, when Nordstrom opened its first East Coast store in Tysons Corner, Virginia, about 90 experienced Nordstrom department managers moved to Virginia from California, Washington, Oregon, Utah, and Alaska, and more than 300 veteran Nordstrom salespeople volunteered to relocate at their own expense. They were motivated by opportunities to move ahead in the company. They knew that they were involved in building something from the ground up.

Promoting From Within

When Nordstrom expanded into women's apparel in 1963, they hired a well-regarded women's apparel retail specialist for their new operation and at least at first: "We marveled at him. He was just what we thought a dress buyer ought to be," Bruce Nordstrom told *Forbes* magazine in 1978. "But one day we were having a meeting to plan our normal sales contest and we said, 'All right, the winners get steak and the losers get beans.' Well, I was walking out behind this guy and he turned to someone and said, 'This is the most sophomoric thing I've ever heard.' I guess it was, but he was at the bottom of all our performance lists. He's a substantial guy in the industry, but he was not for us."

From then on, Nordstrom instituted a policy of never hiring managers from other companies. The danger of hiring and promoting from within is that it can lead to uniform thinking. Nordstrom, however, believes that only people who have started at the bottom and worked their way up through the system can have a full appreciation of the company's unique culture.

In the 1960s, as Nordstrom began its ambitious expansion, the company created a fast career track for up-and-coming employees. Some became buyers in their early twenties; one store manager was just 23; one shoe buyer was a mere 20. Nordstrom continues to find ways to attract good people and keep them motivated with opportunities to ascend the corporate ladder.

It's not uncommon for people who started on the sales floor or in the stockroom to stay with the company for 20 years or more, taking on new assignments as they grow. The majority of leaders began their careers on the sales floor.

In addition, the Rack offers many people a first-time employment opportunity. It's also a great experience during which department managers, store managers, and people in other key positions can grow as leaders.

"The Rack experience reminds you of the importance of team, and the importance of each player being the best at their position," said a regional manager. "You must surround yourself with the best people, articulate the expectations, and then let them soar."

Some of Nordstrom's most successful people have the most experiences, but not necessarily the most experience.

Steve Wilkos, winner of the company's highest honor—the John W. Nordstrom Award—tells new employees: "Try to learn a little bit from a lot of different people. Sometimes we get too locked in to working for a certain leader or particular division. You don't get well rounded that way. I believe the more people you can work for at Nordstrom, the better off you'll be.

"Your career at Nordstrom is yours to build. There really are no rules. That's a tough thing for a lot of people to understand. Most people miss it, because they're looking for this big magical system. It's not there. It's literally 'come in, be yourself, take care of the customer and have some fun.' If you can do that, you can do anything you want in this company."

Indeed, in its messages to new employees, Nordstrom encourages them to have fun, adding, "Fashion is one of the truest forms of self-expression. It's creative and colorful and totally limitless. If you're passionate about fashion, this is the place for you."

A department manager gathers her forces around her when she's coaching them. She tells them: "Let's be a team. I'll show you how I multiple sell, how I suggestive sell. If you have two customers, turn the sitting room into a party. Let them show each other merchandise. Create a fun atmosphere. If you enjoy what you're doing they are going to love it."

As one gung ho salesperson has said, "Even on my bad days I have fun."

With its decentralized system, each division has a life of its own. "If people are carrying out their missions and we feel good about the way they are developing, we will have ourselves new regional managers and buyers as we go into new regions," said Bruce Nordstrom.

"The empowered, decentralized, entrepreneurial spirit of this company has blossomed as the company has grown," said Bruce's son, Erik. "I don't think it would have blossomed if we didn't grow. People wouldn't have seen the opportunities and would not have stayed. There are lots of examples of people who have had great careers with this company. They started on the selling floor and grew with the company. They are the ones who are responsible for our reputation."

The company nurtures the development of employees, and offers a "My Career" website and ongoing coaching feedback.

"We view career development as a shared responsibility among managers, employers, and the company," said Peter Nordstrom. "Our approach is to enable our leaders to be the teachers as well as the developers of their people's growth."

New Employees in New Markets

As Nordstrom has expanded across America, the company faces a constant challenge of finding the kind of people who want to give Nordstrom-like service. When opening a new store, they recruit from within, drawing seasoned Nordies from every region of the company, then hire locals to fill out the staff.

For every 300 or 400 positions that Nordstrom needs to fill in a new store, the company usually receives some 3,000 or 4,000 applicants (a new store in Newark, Delaware, attracted 7,400 applicants); in other words, a person has a 1-in-10 chance of getting hired at Nordstrom.

The people who are not hired are sent thank-you notes because their effort to apply is appreciated and, after all, Nordstrom would like them to remain or become Nordstrom customers.

Initially, Nordstrom doesn't talk a lot about customer service. The company wants potential employees to reflect on their life experiences. What kind of person are you? With the very first interviews, they choose people who were already naturally good at customer service. You can train anyone to do the systems part of it—the register, the ticketing, the merchandise—but you can't teach people to be friendly or great with people.

"In order to provide customers with an experience we can be proud of, we need leaders who can be teachers and mentors so that our new, locally hired salespeople can learn how to 'be' Nordstrom," explained a vice president and regional manager.

At employee orientation, the veteran Nordies speak to new hires about how the company operates. More dramatically, department managers get up and tell their stories about how they started with the company. It isn't just their words. These people are proud of the company and of their accomplishments and so appreciative that they are allowed to prosper. So many people say, "I started with Nordstrom when I was in college and originally it was a part-time job"—10 years later. They might shed a few tears. Sometimes people in the audience are crying along with them. This is how a culture of excellence spreads.

"All the people who work for Nordstrom have this passion about the business," said a new employee. "You really feel that they believe in what they are saying. That's inspiring. When you are sitting there listening to it, you get excited because they are so excited."

In 2004, Robert Spector saw the culture in action during a visit to the then newly opened Nordstrom store in Richmond, Virginia's Short Pump Town Center. A woman, who had been shopping elsewhere in the mall, walked into Nordstrom with large cumbersome packages and boxes and asked a couple of young new male Nordstrom employees if they would help her take the items to her car. The two Nordies happily honored her request. A reporter for the *Richmond Times-Dispatch*, who witnessed this scene, asked the employees why they seized the opportunity to help a woman who had not bought those items in their store. Their answer: "This is Nordstrom." Enough said.

As we will see in the Applications section of this book, when interviewing prospective employees, it is important to ask probing questions to draw out information about applicants' attitudes and aptitude for customer service. Nevertheless, as Blake says: "We don't have a standard set of interview questions. We don't want to be homogenized."

Diversity

"Our people don't have one look, one background, one culture," says Erik. "The common thread is they are themselves. They are genuine."

Nordstrom has had a long standing commitment to increase the minority representation in its general employee and management ranks. It has historically been ranked among the "50 Best Companies for Minorities" in the United States by *Fortune*.

Company policy is to reach out to its communities to recruit, employ, train, and promote ethnic and racial minorities, as well as people with disabilities. The company recruits through targeted media, job fairs, community organizations, and college placement centers.

To recruit workers with disabilities, company representatives attend special job fairs and work with businesses, service agencies, and assistive technology providers who network with the disabled community.

As of 2011, of the company's total employment, 42.2 percent were people of color and 72.1 percent were women. Almost 32 percent of the management population is comprised of people of color and 73 percent are women.

Three people of color and four women serve on the Board of Directors. Chairman Rick Hernandez is Hispanic.

Nordstrom is considered the first upscale retailer to advertise in *Ebony*, a magazine that caters to African-Americans. It also advertises in other publications targeted to people of color, including *Asian*

Enterprise Magazine, Minority Business News USA, Hispanic Business, Black Enterprise, and *Ability.*

Nordstrom regularly features models who reflect the population's various ages, races, and disabilities.

The Human Rights Campaign Foundation, the nation's largest advocacy group of LGBT Americans, gave Nordstrom a perfect score of 100 for the sixth year in a row on its Corporate Equality Index, recognizing the company for creating a workplace that is committed to equality for gay, lesbian, bisexual, and transgender employees.

"What makes this thing work is that it is such a diverse group of people, with all these different experiences," said Blake. "I believe we are the sum of our experiences. How do you hire people with those elements and also get different points of view? That's the challenge. We have to be reflective of our communities and our customer base. We need to encourage different styles and points of view."

Nordstrom has always been a home for ambitious immigrants. Blake points out that a large portion of Nordstrom employees who reach sales of $1 million or more are of foreign extraction. "These people remind my dad [Bruce] of his grandfather [founder John W.], who came to this country from nothing and could barely speak English."

Although all of these top salespeople arrived in the United States with far greater academic credentials than John W., they do share his entrepreneurial spirit.

For example, Van Mensah, the men's suit salesman at the Pentagon City, Virginia, store, is a native of Ghana who holds an MBA degree from Northeastern University in Boston.

In the late 1980s, Mensah was a department manager for home furnishings, fine china, and furniture at the Woodward & Lothrop store in Washington. At that time, Woodward & Lothrop was anxiously preparing for the arrival of its new competitor, Nordstrom, which was opening its first East Coast store at Tysons Corner. Woodward & Lothrop tried to get its employees to act more like Nordstrom employees by showing an instructional video on how Nordstrom operated and how it empowered employees to make decisions.

"That was the first time I had heard about Nordstrom," recalled Mensah. "I thought, 'This would be a nice company to work for.'" He soon left Woodward & Lothrop and joined Nordstrom in 1988 as a member of the original staff at Tysons Corner.

Mensah has been a Pacesetter and a million-dollar seller for many years. As for Woodward & Lothrop, it went out of business in 1996.

Nader Shafii, a native of Tehran, Iran, came to the United States in 1975, and six years later graduated from Eastern Oregon State University. Soon afterward, he moved to Portland, Oregon, where he went to work part-time at Nordstrom's Washington Square store. At the time, he was not considering a career in retail. He was still searching for what he wanted to do with his life.

"On several occasions, I met members of the Nordstrom family at store meetings," he recalls. John, Bruce, and Jim Nordstrom (the group who ran the company from the late 1960s to the mid-1990s), would often "walk around the store and talk to the people on the floor. As a business graduate, I was impressed that the copresidents of the company would talk to the sales staff on the floor and ask questions. It intrigued me. I felt the warmth, the closeness among the managers and staff. You did not feel it was a boss/subordinate relationship. That's when I started to look more seriously at a career in retail. The more I listened to them speak, the more I understood what this company is based on. It changed me from wanting to have a job to having a career. I stayed in retail, specifically at Nordstrom, because of who these people were."

Today, Shafii works in the Personal Touch department at the store in the South Coast Plaza, in Costa Mesa, California.

The Nordies Versus the Clock Punchers ————————————

Despite its strong reputation as an employer, Nordstrom has had problems with certain members of its workforce.

In 1990, Nordstrom found itself in a battle with the union that represented the five original stores in the company's home area of Seattle and Tacoma—the only stores in the chain that were represented by a union. Many veteran employees wanted to make union membership optional; the union was solidly opposed to that proposition and fought it when the contract was up for renewal.

The union engaged in a highly publicized public relations campaign in an effort to harm the company. It never called a strike because it did not have the votes of the rank and file. But the union charged that Nordstrom was not paying employees for hand delivering purchases to customers at their homes or places of business, and was not compensating employees for doing inventory and other tasks.

Ultimately, Nordstrom set up a claims process to deal with complaints of off-the-clock work. Pay practices were changed and a new policy was laid out for employees to record all hours worked. Nordstrom immediately began paying workers for attending store meetings, doing inventory work, and making "hand carries"—picking up merchandise at one store and delivering it to another. If done during regular work hours, hand carries would be covered as part of an employee's selling hours, which determine sales-per-hour performance. Recording this additional hour was a disincentive for top salespeople because vacation pay was determined by sales-per-hour results. Other deliveries that were made to help the department would be considered "non-sell" hours, and would not affect sales-per-hour performance. (Employees would receive an hourly wage for that time.) When making deliveries going to or from work, pay would be calculated over and above the regular commute time. The same criteria would apply to a salesperson's delivery to a customer's home, office, or hotel. A few pages expanded the Nordstrom rulebook, at least metaphorically.

Many enterprising salespeople disagreed in principle with being paid specifically for deliveries made to their personal customers. Customer service means being there when the customer needs you. The structure gives the salesperson more flexibility with the customer, and the payoff is always going to be there. On one typical day, before her shift began, a salesperson drove to another Portland-area Nordstrom to pick up a dress for a customer who had to attend a funeral, and then drove back to the Washington Square store where she handed over the garment to the deeply appreciative customer. Later that day, the salesperson delivered another dress to a customer who needed it by a certain time but couldn't get to the store. Those kinds of heroics make Nordstrom look even better in the customers' eyes.

The people who do the best for the company (and themselves) are the ones who respond to the system, work the hardest, and do what it takes to be more productive. There still has to be room to allow salespersons to be the best they can be, to take the initiative to do the extra things. What's wrong with writing thank-you notes at home on your own time, or getting the walls stocked to make your area easier to sell in? It will make your income better. A salesperson says, "I do get paid for that type of work; my commissions prove it. It's ludicrous to be forced to pay someone to sit down and write a thank-you note. How do you make someone be nice to a customer?"

Good Place to Work

Nordstrom has consistently been selected as one of the 100 Best Companies to Work for in America. More than several thousand employees have been with the company for longer than 10 years. It is among the top 50 companies in the United States based on wages of women corporate officers, who constitute more than 40 percent of corporate officers.

Company literature tells employees: "It's your business: Our employees have a personal, financial, and professional stake in the success of our company. You're encouraged to take ownership of your career."

Nordstrom has set up a compensation system to help employees achieve personal wealth. The company has a generous 401(k) plan as well as profit sharing and an employee stock-purchase plan.

Like everything else at Nordstrom, the profit-sharing plan has built-in financial incentives that encourage industriousness, teamwork, customer service, and expense savings. Because contributions are made to the plan directly from the company's net earnings, employees have an incentive to be productive and cost-conscious. (Nordstrom's shrinkage rate—losses due to employee theft—is only 1 percent of sales, which is half the industry average.) That also promotes loyalty because employees share ownership.

"If you are part of our team, the number-one thing you have is your integrity, character, and reputation," says Blake. "You have a vested interest in the success of this company. So, if you see that something is not right, you will speak up and make it right."

Today, some longtime employees retire with profit-sharing totals in the high six figures. All employees who work more than a thousand hours per year and are still actively employed at the end of the year participate in the plan.

Hiring for Customer Service

Whenever the three Nordstrom brothers (often accompanied by their cousin, Jamie, President of Nordstrom Direct, the Internet and Catalog division) attend the opening of a new Nordstrom store, they meet individually with new employees to explain the history and guiding principles of the company. One key topic, of course, is customer service.

When they ask new employee teams why the company places such a high priority on service, they often get back answers such as "It builds customer loyalty" or "It's part of the Nordstrom reputation."

Writing in the employee publication, *Loop,* the Nordstrom brothers said: "The single most important reason we try to provide great service is this: It enables us to sell more. Over the years we've learned that the best way for our company to achieve results is to do what's best for the customer. While that may sound simple, it's easier said than done. It's easy to get caught up in the day-to-day activities and not focus enough on the outcomes we're seeking. The ultimate filter for all our efforts should be: *How is this meaningful to the customer and will it increase sales?*"

3

Nurture the Nordie

Mentor, Support, Praise, Recognize, and Reward

When we hire those eager beavers, it would be a crime if we didn't feed them while they're hungry.

—Bruce Nordstrom

Nordstrom is an organization fueled by emotions. Motivated employees bring a passion to their business, a drive to succeed, a desire to sell, and a long-term devotion to serving the customer.

Managers and buyers, who are charged with bringing out the best in each member of their team, work to sustain this spirit by creating an emotional bond with their fellow employees through a potent blend of praise, recognition, and joy. And occasionally even tears.

"Sometimes we push you, sometimes we pat you on the back," said a national merchandise manager for one of Nordstrom's shoe divisions. "When I was a store manager, I wouldn't ask anyone to do something that I wouldn't do, whether stacking merchandise for a sale, or staying late. I tell people to be accountable for what you do; work hard, and you can do whatever you want to do.

"You can't tell someone to go out and give good customer service, to go out and get a sales increase. You have to tell them how to do it. Give the salespeople something they can use. For example, suggest that they send a thank-you note to a customer who brought back a return."

After going through employee orientation and becoming familiar with the culture, the systems, the merchandise, and the sales goals expectations, salespeople are encouraged and empowered to develop their own style, to find their own niche, their own way of taking care of business that fits their unique personality and talents because, ultimately, success at Nordstrom comes down to what works for each individual. Not everybody can be a top seller, but everybody has certain strengths.

Although this book is entitled *The Nordstrom Way*, there are actually more than 50,000 Nordstrom ways, because each employee is an individual, with a unique style and approach to taking care of the customer. To achieve the top levels of sales performance, salespeople must take the requisite time and have the patience to gradually develop a personal clientele.

Each new salesperson is matched with an experienced salesperson or manager from his or her department for up to a full day of observation and practice. They work through a checklist of selling concepts and role-playing scenarios to help bridge the gap between the new hire's first day on the job and another class, 45 days later, called "Selling Is Service," where they learn the foundation of selling at Nordstrom, how to develop expert fashion knowledge, and how to confidently engage with the customer. They are taught "relationship selling," which creates a positive experience for the customer.

Top salespeople believe in making customers their best friends. Customers are there to spend money, so make them happy.

Product Knowledge

You can't develop a relationship with a customer if you don't know your product.

Product knowledge is power. Salespeople should know everything about the item—the raw materials, the cut, the fit, the previous version, and so on, because it gives them credibility with the customer. Because a good salesperson must be current with product specifications, style changes, fashion trends, and other industry information, Nordstrom offers them seminars, demonstrations, videos, and, occasionally, firsthand looks at how the products are constructed.

Salespeople promote product features, advantages, and benefits to match the customer's expressed needs and wants. Nordstrom mandates that salespeople promote "fit first" because if the product doesn't fit, nothing else matters.

"The more you know, the better you can serve your customer," said a personal stylist in Northern California: "In men's clothing we go through a fit certification program, so we're able to identify the right garment for each body part."

Top Nordstrom salespeople do not confine their product knowledge to their own department. By learning about the products in other departments, they take advantage of a Nordstrom policy that empowers salespeople to sell anything in any department throughout the store. (We go into that aspect of the culture in more detail in Chapter 4: Empower Entrepreneurs to Own the Customer Experience.)

To best serve their customers, salespeople must be aware of what's new in departments throughout the store, not just in their own department. For example, a women's wear department manager on the East Coast uses the services of a variety of specialists from tailors to certified shoe fitters and fit specialists in lingerie, who are trained to exacting standards.

"I always ask my customers how long it's been since they've been fitted for a bra," said the manager. "If she has never been fitted, I'll introduce her to one of our specialists. If she's recently been fitted and knows her size, I'll run upstairs and ask our salespeople what's hot and new, so I can find the perfect bra or underpinning to complete her look. Those extra steps bring customers back to you. You may spend several hours with one person, but you're serving all her needs and making her feel special. The next time she needs a gift or something to wear to a party, she'll think of you first. That's when you have a customer for life."

Salespeople are asked to provide immediate feedback to the department manager on the quality, construction, fit, and availability of every product they sell, so that the manager can respond accordingly. This is communication, which we will delve into deeper in Chapter 6, Communication and Teamwork: We're All in the Customer Service Department.

A Nordie must be able to get excited about the product, said a salesperson. "If you're not interested, why would you expect the customer to be interested? Why should I buy something from a salesperson who doesn't care?"

Appreciation Promotes Motivation

Managers at every level work hard to make sure that their colleagues know that they are appreciated. John Whitacre, the late chairman, used to tell managers that twice a day, for 60 seconds, they should look a fellow employee in the eye and tell him or her how much the manager cares about that employee, and the reasons why.

A store manager in California helps new department heads find mentor-managers through a variety of ways, including brainstorming sessions. "I might do a managers' meeting where somebody is really great in a particular area, such as planning special events or helping other people achieve their goals. That would give other managers ideas."

A store manager in the Pacific Northwest makes sure that he knows the names and the faces of everybody who works in his store. "Being able to praise people is so important. It's the simple, personal things you say about them. You walk up to a salesperson and you say, 'I saw you had a 15 percent increase yesterday. Good job!' That's powerful. You need to point out to others what makes that person a unique member of his or her department."

This is especially true for new hires, because starting from scratch as a Nordstrom salesperson can be an intimidating experience. One is surrounded by ambitious, motivated entrepreneurs who want to succeed and advance. What's more, those veterans already have their own clientele.

So, how does a new salesperson get customers? The old-fashioned way: one at a time. Call your friends, call your relatives. Call the friends of your relatives and the relatives of your friends. Be proactive. Be entrepreneurial. Exploit your advantages and talents.

When a Mexican-American salesperson began building up her business in San Diego, she took advantage of her contacts in the local Mexican-American community. Her ability to speak Spanish "comes in handy and can really be an advantage."

A similar challenge is faced by Nordstrom employees who open stores in regions of the country where Nordstrom had not previously been. Often these pioneering employees don't have the luxury of calling on friends or relatives to help them develop their business. They must find other ways to build up their clientele one person at a time. They develop a personal book of customer data, including purchases and preferences, send thank-you notes, make a lot of phone calls, and work hard at developing long-term relationships with customers.

Like competitive athletes, Nordstrom salespeople are motivated in a variety of ways to give extraordinary service because that kind of service produces extraordinary sales volumes. The company regularly distributes video interviews with top salespeople, who are encouraged to pass on the knowledge and tricks they have acquired along the way, such as goal setting, marketing, selling by using the phone, and, of course, giving great customer service. That is how a customer service, sales-oriented culture is perpetuated and sustained. Those successful salespeople were once mentored by other successful salespeople. And so it goes.

Also, frequent staff meetings serve as workshops for salespeople to compare, examine, and discuss sales techniques, and to perform skits in which they play the roles of salesperson and customer.

Mentoring

Because Nordstrom management understands the challenges of the sales floor, they empower managers at every level to nurture the career paths of the people they are supervising. This nurturing begins with mentoring new employees.

Mentorship starts with the store manager, who, in each store, is the embodiment of Nordstrom culture. Many store managers develop their own individual mentoring programs based on the needs of their employees. They are also responsible for supporting these nascent Nordies in their efforts; praising them and recognizing their accomplishments at every opportunity; and rewarding them for a job well done.

"You can observe a lot just by watching," Yogi Berra once said. That's why new employees are encouraged to watch, observe, and ask questions. That's an often-overlooked element of empowerment.

"Over the years, we've done more and more mentoring for people at the entry level," said Bruce Nordstrom. "Newcomers get a quick understanding of what we're trying to do, but some of them don't buy into it. If you lay it out for them, via a mentor, the people who have it within themselves are more apt to buy into our deal."

Inspirational mentors transfer that culture to new Nordstrom associates. That's how this company has been able to thrive for more than a century, through four generations of management.

"We want our good people, our proven performers, to be nice and helpful to new people," Bruce wrote in his memoir. "Unfortunately, some of the real star salespeople don't want to mentor. They get protective of their turf and don't want to cut anybody in on it. Rather than waste their time helping someone else, they'd rather spend all their time on their own production. Fortunately, most top salespeople are more apt to be team players."

One of those team players was David Butler, a now retired, top-performing shoe salesman from the Tacoma store.

As he was winding down his career at Nordstrom, "being number one was not as important to me as it used to be," said Butler. "It would have been very selfish of me not to share with other people what I was able to accomplish. I tried to help teach others what it takes to become a Pacesetter [top-selling performer] and give them the tools to do it. It was a lot more fun for me helping the entire department make their day, which helped the store make its day."

When Patrick McCarthy joined Nordstrom in 1971, he soon realized that he needed a mentor to teach him how to survive. He eventually found his role model in a coworker named Ray Black, who was a professional menswear salesman. Thoroughly knowledgeable about the merchandise, Black could take a swatch from a bolt of fabric that was going to be tailored for a suit and coordinate a complete wardrobe of shirts and ties, all the way down to the cuff links.

Before joining Nordstrom, Black had worked for many years in several of downtown Seattle's fine specialty menswear shops, and his loyal clients followed him from store to store. "They came into the department asking for Ray because he identified their needs and knew how to satisfy them," McCarthy recalled. "Men saw him as an ally. They heeded his advice on where to get a good haircut or what style of glasses to wear. He offered them choices and suggestions and gave them the confidence to try something different. Their wives saw Ray as the mediator who could interpret their views to their husbands."

McCarthy also noticed that Black had the ability to remember not only a customer's name but his last purchase as well. (This was long before previous purchases became part of the store's computerized database.)

"I thought to myself, 'I want to be able to do that.'" So, McCarthy volunteered to help Black whenever and wherever Black needed him, and the veteran salesman accepted the offer. "Pretty soon, we developed a routine: After Ray sold suits and sport coats to his customers, I helped them with their shirts and ties. With that increased customer contact, I was able to develop my poise and improve my interviewing skills."

Most importantly, Black taught McCarthy how to become an entrepreneur who could create his own business.

Black didn't sit around waiting for people to walk into the menswear department; he called customers on the phone to alert them to new merchandise that was arriving in the store. "Ray showed me what a good salesman should be; he showed me that the Nordstrom system worked and that I could make as much money as I wanted," McCarthy recalled. "The way I saw it, the Nordstroms were taking all of the risks and providing all of the ingredients—the nice stores, the ambiance, the high-quality merchandise—to make it work. All I had to do was arrive every morning prepared to give an honest day's work and to value and honor the customer."

Over the rest of his career, as McCarthy rose to the top of the Nordstrom mountain, he became a mentor to many employees.

Van Mensah, who sells men's suits in the Pentagon City, Virginia, store, said that "Patrick McCarthy told me: 'Don't reinvent the wheel. Focus on winning one customer at a time. Be honest and sincere. Do what's right. There's nothing magical about this.' That's been my guiding principle. To make it work, you have to live it every day. Make it your mind-set."

Mensah has gone on to become one of Nordstrom's top salespeople and he, in turn, has become a mentor. "When we have a new store opening, I have been asked to fly in to meet with the salespeople in the menswear area to talk about how to build a successful business," said Mensah.

Mensah believes that honesty and sincerity are the keys to success.

"When you are dealing with the kind of clients who come to Nordstrom, if you try to play games, they will see through that very quickly," he said. "If you know the merchandise is not right, come forward and say, 'in my professional opinion, this is not going to work for what you are buying it for.' You might lose some money; it might be the most expensive item he wants to buy. But I would rather sell him something that is less expensive but will actually work better for him. If you tell him the product is not right for him, you get more credibility."

Similarly, a women's wear department manager in the Midwest says the first step in creating a relationship is earning the customer's trust. "My favorite line is, 'I don't make the clothes, so you don't have to like my suggestions. I'm just telling you what I think you should have.' I love it when I get a customer to try something a little out of the box and they look and feel fabulous. That really helps build their confidence in me. We're not just selling them clothes, we're building their self-esteem."

Van Mensah's reputation among the Washington power elite earned him a place in the Pentagon's Executive Transitional Assistance Program, which helps soon-to-be-retired senior officers—generals, colonels—learn how to transition into civilian life. Van conducts the "professional image" segment of the program for these officers, who are brought into Washington from military bases around the world. Mensah frequently gets follow-up calls from these officers who need a suit for a meeting or a job interview.

When it comes to selling suits to congressmen and senators, Mensah is strictly bipartisan. He was given presidential cufflinks by a former cabinet member, and was invited to George W. Bush's presidential inaugural in 2001 by a former senator who was on the transition committee.

Asked to describe his proudest moment working at Nordstrom, Mensah recalled the time he received a phone call from a customer who had rushed to get a flight to Washington for a wedding, only to discover that he had somehow packed the pants from one suit and the jacket from another suit. "Van," said the customer over his cell phone, "I'm in big trouble."

Because Van knew the customer's size, he made sure a new suit was ready—including alterations—when the customer arrived at the store, with his limousine waiting. Not only that, Van noticed the customer's belt looked old, so Van sold him a new belt. Fifteen minutes later, the customer was on his way to the wedding.

That's how a culture is sustained, by passing on the knowledge from one employee to another.

Recognition and Praise

"There are two things people want more than sex and money," Mary Kay Ash, founder of Mary Kay Cosmetics, has said. "Those two things are recognition and praise."

"Recognition and praise are the best motivators I know," said a Pacific Northwest store manager. "When you recognize and praise your people, they will go out and do anything for you. Every time you talk to me you're going to hear me talk about my team and how wonderful they are, and what they did."

Recognition is powerful, as long as it's authentic and specific. Whatever their level on the inverted pyramid, employees wants to feel needed and valued.

One of the greatest and simplest forms of recognition is just to walk up to a salesperson and thank her for a job well done. When you tell her that a customer took the time to call or to write a letter about her, that means a lot. By recognizing those people, Nordstrom reinforces the meaning of the inverted pyramid—front-line people are important because they are the ones who take care of the customer every single day.

Nordstrom reinforced that idea on the cover of its 2009 annual report to shareholders by quoting a long handwritten letter from a customer in Las Vegas praising one employee:

Once again, I must give a standing ovation to my favorite Nordstrom guy, Bryan Sportell. I visited Nordstrom and returned home with four more pairs of shoes. Bryan's level of customer service exceeds my expectations every time! He remembers my name, my shoe size, and my brand preference and always guides me toward shoes that will actually fit comfortably and suit my particular style needs.

In addition to Bryan's expertise in finding the perfect shoe for his client, his engaging personality makes it a real pleasure to hand over my Nordstrom charge card for each sale!

I make a point to shop on days when I know Bryan will be working, as I wouldn't consider going to anyone else to make this type of purchase. My closet is filled with dozens of pairs of Nordstrom shoes, which is an homage to his ability to please his clients.

In this day and age when everyone is so anxious to complain about everything, I wanted to take the opportunity to let you know that one of your great staff is doing everything perfectly! Bravo, Bryan!

Now, that's recognition and praise writ large.

Every year, the company gives a variety of awards including those for the best-performing regional and national merchandisers, buyers, retail directors, loss prevention and logistics people. The Customer Service Manager of the Year has the best overall performance in expenses, sales, bad debt reduction, credit participation, support of new company selling, and leadership. The Customer Service Book Award is given to the store with the letters that show the greatest service impact, not necessarily the store with the largest quantity of letters. Nordstrom executives read all the letters that come in from customers and attach notes for the store managers to review. Managers send notes to those people for a job well done.

Recognition Meetings

One venue for reinforcing, recognizing, and rewarding behavior is the monthly Recognition Meeting, which is a feature of the Nordstrom culture.

At a typical Recognition Meeting in the downtown Seattle flagship store, smartly dressed men and women enter the John W. Nordstrom Room, where the company holds its annual shareholders' meeting and other large gatherings. It's 7:30 in the morning. Pulsating disco music blares over the speaker system and colleagues hug each other like long-lost friends. The energy is infectious. Some people bring pom-poms, clappers, flags, and even bullhorns to create a celebratory atmosphere.

Decorative yellow balloons are everywhere as these several hundred managers and salespeople find their way to their seats. Throughout the room are signs emphasizing customer service, such as:

We built this business one customer at a time.
Our customer service relationship is a fragile proposition. It's not elastic.
The question we should always be asking ourselves is this: Is the customer having
an exceptional experience?

By eight o'clock sharp, they are all in their seats, in sections reserved for the eight stores in the Pacific Northwest region, representing Washington state and Alaska.

An observer can't help but be caught up in the spirit of the event, which is almost like a pageant. While the surface objective is to recognize outstanding sales performance, the meeting is also used to rally the troops and to get everyone excited about the performance of their teammates in their department, their store, their region, and their company.

"These meetings are probably the biggest morale boosters in our company because they double as pep rallies," said Bruce. "The people who attend these meetings get so charged up, they take that energy back to their departments and it spreads throughout the company."

Employees and stores are singled out for categories such as departmental sales increases and promotional ideas that drive sales increases. Also honored are departments that have sold the most of that particular month's featured item. Nordstrom loves to use inter-company competition as a tool for motivating the troops. (More about that in Chapter 5: Compensate According to Results.)

Managers are there to inspire. As one manager said at a Recognition Meeting: "Every time a customer comes into our store is an opportunity to create a memory. We need to staff our store with memory makers."

Store and department managers select Customer Service All-Stars, in sales and support roles and rewards them with incentives such as cash and gifts and recognition.

Customer Service All-Stars involved in sales are selected based on three criteria: sales volume, consistent customer service, and teamwork—the level of support they give their coworkers. These All-Stars are given a 33 percent store discount (rather than the traditional 20 percent) for one year, special business cards recognizing their achievement, and an All-Star pin to wear. Their photos are displayed in the Customer Service department of their store for the next year, and their names and photos appear in *Loop*, the employee newsletter. They also get the shift that works best for them. Some prefer the busiest times; others opt for shifts that coordinate with their personal lives.

Adding some emotional drama to the proceedings, these All-Stars are not told in advance that they are being honored. However, Nordstrom does notify their parents and/or spouse and children, whom Nordstrom secretly brings to the meeting—unbeknownst to the honoree.

Imagine that you are an honoree. You are called out of the audience and you bound up to the front of the room for a standing ovation in front of your peers. Then from stage left, you see Mom and Dad or Grandma and Grandpa, or the wife and kids, who are sharing this emotional moment with you. There's not a dry eye in the house. You feel like running through the doors of the room and selling a woman a pair of red pumps!

All-Stars and their families pose for pictures, then get together for a breakfast after the meeting.

At a recent Recognition Meeting, Dan Brator, of the Bellevue Square store east of Seattle, was selected as the Building Services Support All-Star. A Nordstrom employee for more than three decades in sales, he later moved to support, "where he maintains the integrity of the building, and takes care of us—his customers," said Brator's store manager.

Also at Recognition Meetings, customers' letters of appreciation are read and positive achievements are recognized, while coworkers stand up and cheer for each other.

For example, here's one about a salesperson from the East Coast. A customer wrote: "I am deaf, and I wanted slippers for my mother. I left the old slippers in my other car." The salesperson called the woman's husband for her (she couldn't use the phone), "got the size, and talked him into shopping for dinner, and cooking it."

A good Recognition Meeting encompasses four key aspects:

1. Demonstrate sincere, authentic appreciation for the people you are honoring. You need to talk about the essence of what a person does; what makes her different; how she adds value.
2. Emphasize the team spirit. Nordstrom wants its people to feel that they work for a great company in the world, the greatest region in the greatest company in the world; the best division/best department. Part of the culture is competition. You can use that as a weapon. Where does our region rank within the company?
3. Teach people something new, such as sales techniques or promotional ideas. Show motivational videos, skits, and performances.
4. Perpetuate the culture. Discuss key points about the culture. Reinforce what makes Nordstrom unique and how the culture works for them.

John W. Nordstrom Award

The highest recognition at Nordstrom is winning the John W. Nordstrom (JWN) Award, which goes to the manager who most exemplifies the characteristics of the founder, which the company lists as "hard work, persistence, servant leadership, loyalty, honesty, ethics' competitive spirit, and an unwavering commitment to putting the customer first."

John W. Nordstrom's great-grandsons, Blake, Peter, Erik, and Jamie, solicit nominations from regional managers, who in turn request them from store managers. Generating good sales numbers is one major criterion, but the winner must also be a selfless team player and committed to doing business the Nordstrom Way.

The identity of the winner is known only to the handful of people who will keep it a surprise until it's announced at a regularly scheduled regional Recognition Meeting. Nordstrom likes to add a little drama to the proceedings, for maximum impact.

While the regional manager conducts the meeting, all of a sudden the Nordstrom great-grandsons make their surprise entrance. The employees erupt as if The Beatles had just shown up. Everybody knows that something special is going to happen. The winner is announced, springs up to the front of the room, and here comes his or her spouse and children to share the moment. Tears and laughter. And the ultimate recognition.

Each year, new and past winners of the JWN Award attend a dinner in Seattle, hosted by the Nordstrom family. The company pays for travel and lodging for the winners and their guests, whether or not they're still working for the company.

Everyday Praise

When individuals and departments have a successful day or are on target in reaching their sales goals, they are praised over the store intercom during the morning announcements before the store opens.

The company announces group and individual awards for categories such as outstanding sales-per-hour and sales-per-month performances.

"We are at our best when we recognize good performance," Bruce wrote in his memoir. "Recognition and praise are heartfelt and personal. That recognition is better than a vacation in Hawaii. We put people in front of their peers and tell them that they are the kind of person we want others to emulate. We tell them we value and cherish their input to this company, and we wouldn't be as successful without that individual. That's strong stuff.

"Why are we constantly finding ways to praise and recognize our people? Because selling is tough. Sometimes you're dealing with angry and complaining customers who are yelling at you. Believe me, I know from experience. We have so many good folks who have made careers of this, and it's up to us to provide them some uplift as they work day after day, week after week, year after year."

Letters of complaint about Nordstrom's customer service (omitting the names of the offending salespeople) are also read over the store intercom. "That's how we learn that the customer is our boss," said Patrick McCarthy. "Nordstrom's name is on my paycheck, but I'm paid by the customer."

Heroics: Inspirational Tales of Teamwork and Legendary Customer Service

"We like to tell stories around here," said Erik Nordstrom. "Not a day goes by when the three of us don't communicate with customers."

Reflecting the company's inverted pyramid, Nordstrom's philosophy is that neither "corporate" nor "leadership" creates the Nordstrom story; employees and customers do. Storytelling and folklore play a critical role in spreading Nordstrom's values and priorities throughout every level, department, and region.

Stories of customer service and teamwork above and beyond the call of duty have their own word at Nordstrom: "heroics." When a Nordstrom employee witnesses a coworker providing great service—whether to a customer or a colleague—he or she is encouraged to write up what that coworker has done and submit it to the department or store manager, who will publicly praise that employee. The best stories are disseminated and shared through as many internal corporate communication channels as possible—verbally, digitally, and in print.

Heroics are an essential feature of the Nordstrom Way because they demonstrate and illustrate qualities of teamwork and customer service that ultimately produce sales. Heroics are an ideal way to pass on the company's cultural values, to serve as reminders of the level of service to which all employees should aspire or surpass. They also allow employees to recognize fellow employees for the special lengths they go to for a customer (who may never know what that "heroic" employee did).

"There is nothing so nice as doing good by stealth and being found out by accident," wrote Charles Lamb, the English essayist.

By sharing these heroics, Nordstrom management honors and salutes employees who go above and beyond the call of duty, which sends the message that customer service—both internally and externally—is what makes Nordstrom Nordstrom.

Frequent subjects of the heroics are selected as Customer Service All-Stars with their pictures mounted in the customer service area in the store where they work.

The cumulative effect of this continual reinforcement at Nordstrom is that the front-line workers get it. They understand that the people who run Nordstrom single out, honor, and reward outstanding acts of customer service, and that the way to advance in the company is to give great customer service. If you see a great example, you're going to imitate that.

There are many examples of heroics. For example, there is the story of a customer who fell in love with a pair of burgundy pleated Donna Karan slacks that had recently gone on sale at the Nordstrom store in downtown Seattle. But the store was out of her size, and the salesperson was unable to track down a pair at the five other Nordstrom stores in the Seattle area. Aware that the same slacks were available across the street at a competitor, the salesperson secured some petty cash from her department manager, marched across the street to a competing retailer, where she bought the slacks (at full price), returned to Nordstrom, and then sold them to the customer for the marked-down Nordstrom price.

Obviously, Nordstrom didn't make money on that sale, but it was an investment in promoting the loyalty of an appreciative customer, who thought of Nordstrom for her next purchase.

4

Empower Entrepreneurs to Own the Customer Experience

We've never tried to solve a customer service challenge from a meeting room at headquarters or through training modules and policies. We've always done it through empowerment— and that's the only way we're going to meet the challenge today.

—Erik Nordstrom

If you boil the Nordstrom system down to its essence, down to the one sentence that separates Nordstrom from most other companies, it is this: Nordstrom gives its people on the sales floor—the front line of the business—the freedom to make entrepreneurial decisions, and management backs them on those decisions. Everything else flows from that simple premise.

That's called empowerment. In most businesses, it's a cliché. At Nordstrom, it's a reality.

"We believe in empowering people as close to the customer as we can, in order for those people to bring an entrepreneurial, proprietary attitude to their business," said Bruce. "You have to be confident enough in your system and your people to take your hands off and allow business to work."

Geevy Thomas, president of the Rack division, has said, "There are three groups of people with respect to empowerment: Those who get it. Those who really want to get it. Those who probably will never get it."

Nordstrom has no official mission statement or value statement. Blake said, "It's clear throughout our organization that our people are empowered to use their energy and their entrepreneurial spirit to take care of the customer."

That's it.

The company unendingly reinforces that sense of empowerment. If an employee wants to go above and beyond for a customer or would like to make a suggestion on how to improve service or to try something new, "We want you to take the initiative," company literature says, "and we'll support your efforts to deliver exceptional service."

At Nordstrom, "Selling something is the best service that we can provide."

Take, for example, this story of employee initiative. An employee from a Nordstrom store in the Midwest wrote this note praising one of her coworkers in a women's fashion department, whom we will call Jane:

"Recently, a couple from New Hampshire stopped in Studio 121 and Jane helped them. The wife tried on a red jacket with matching sweater and looked fabulous. Her husband kept telling her to buy them, but she hesitated even though she loved them.

"Jane questioned the customer about her hesitation. The customer told her they were in from out of town for a party, and she hadn't brought her jewelry. Jane asked whether the customer liked the necklace and earrings that Jane herself was wearing, and the customer replied 'yes.' Jane offered to loan them for the evening. The customer bought the jacket and sweater and when Jane wrapped the purchases she also wrapped her jewelry to go with them. The couple was staying close to where Jane's son works, so she gave them directions to drop off her jewelry with him. The jewelry was returned along with a very gracious thank-you note."

Nordstrom empowers salespeople and managers at all levels with a wide range of operational and bottom-line responsibilities (such as controlling costs), without shackling them with lots of bureaucratic guidelines that get in the way of serving the customer. This way, Nordstrom allows its people to operate like nimble entrepreneurial shopkeepers rather than static blocks in a retailing monolith.

"We stand when the customer stands," said a top salesperson in a women's sportswear department in the Midwest. "We're on the floor where the customer sits. And we strive to serve one customer at a time."

To help front-line people take ownership of their business and to build it up into a thriving enterprise, the company gives them the necessary tools, such as inviting stores, ample merchandise, state-of-the-art inventory and replenishment systems, computerized personal books, thank-you notes, and so much more.

In a State of the Company address, Blake said, "If everyone can feel like it's their reputation, it's their name on the door, and that they are in an environment that values them, trusts them, hears them, and allows them to make a difference, then collectively we have a great chance of succeeding."

That's how Nordstrom gets comments like this, from a women's sportswear salesperson in the Seattle area: "It may say Nordstrom on the front of the building, but I want the customer, when she thinks of Nordstrom, to think of *me*. I believe the department where I work is *my* franchise. This company gives you the freedom to help the customer with everything. No one tells you that there's only one way to do your business. Nordstrom lets you do whatever it takes to make the customer happy, as long as it's legal. They are not going to say 'no' to you if the end result is a happy customer."

And from this women's apparel salesperson in New Jersey: "We do the little things that other retailers don't do—like locating an item from another store, checking on Direct-To-Customer [mail order] deliveries, setting up the dressing room, and escorting the customer to different departments. I've learned to approach customer service as if I'm running my own store. As a shop owner, you would greet every customer. You would learn their names and keep in touch with them. You would also go the extra mile. A couple of times I have hand delivered alterations to a customer's home. They were really wowed by that."

No employee at Nordstrom is beneath doing a little housekeeping. That includes people named Nordstrom.

A woman who had worked at Nordstrom in the 1980s told Robert Spector a story about Bruce Nordstrom walking through her department one day. Bruce spotted a can of soda on the counter. He picked up the can, deposited it in a wastebasket, and continued on his way. He didn't ask who was responsible for the can being on the counter and he didn't order an employee to take it away. He just did it himself. This woman, who went on to run several of her own successful businesses, never forgot the day that she saw the chairman of the company set an example for her—without his even uttering a word.

Ideas From Empowered Entrepreneurs

"The great ideas never come from the executive office," said a Nordstrom executive. "The great ideas come from the floor."

Great new ideas emerge when employees feel empowered to offer suggestions on how to do their job better and more efficiently.

Nordstrom has an Innovation Team comprised of a small group of executives who rely on front-line employees to suggest well-thought-out ideas about improvements that would make business sense. Employees submit a one-page form that explains their idea and makes the case for its implementation. The Innovation Team reviews the ideas and decides which merit funding. If an idea has value, Nordstrom quickly tests it.

For example, front-line employees suggested that stores be equipped with Wi-Fi for the implementation of Mobile Point Of Sale (POS) devices, which enable salespeople to do a variety of tasks, including searching for merchandise throughout the company's inventory system, and freeing customers to make purchases in any location in the store instead of only at a cash register. "In my area, it gets really crowded by the register," said a salesperson in the Northeast. "I love being able to get the customer away from the crowd."

Here's another example of an idea that came from the front lines: A menswear salesman was about to assist a couple of shoppers who knew no English. He took out his smartphone, which had a language translation app, and used it to first greet the customers, then to sell them several items. The salesman's store manager shared that story with her store's sales information manager, who in turn shared it with colleagues in their region. As a result, the Google Translate App was installed on the iPads and iPhones of other salespeople in the stores in the region.

Empowered to Take Ownership of the Customer Experience

A woman customer was shopping at the Nordstrom store at the South Park mall in Charlotte, North Carolina. It was near closing time. She tried on some clothes, made some purchases and went directly home. That night, before going to bed, she discovered that a 2.8-carat diamond from her wedding ring was missing. She assumed that she lost the diamond at Nordstrom.

The very next morning, she came to the store when it opened and headed over to the women's department, where she had last been. She got down on her hands and knees, searching for the diamond.

Eric Wilson, the Loss Prevention agent for that store, noticed the customer crawling on the floor, and asked how he could help. After she explained the situation to him, Eric got down on his hands and knees and joined the search. No luck. He took the customer's contact information and told her he would follow up.

Eric then contacted two employees in Building Services, Bart Garcia and Tom Fraley, who joined in the search. Again, no luck. Perhaps the diamond was in one of the vacuum cleaner bags? They gathered the vacuum bags, and began splitting them open and sifting through their dirty contents. Eventually, voilà! They found the diamond.

When Eric called the customer to tell her the good news, she was thrilled to the point of tears. Soon after, her sister blogged about the experience, and others tweeted their appreciation for the team's service.

Clearly, Eric Wilson took the initiative. His job description did not include scrutinizing full vacuum cleaner bags. He could have told Building Services about the lost diamond and then moved on with his tasks for the day. But the customer wanted someone to find her diamond. Eric owned the situation. He figured out the best approach to solving the problem and made a difference in a person's life.

The tale of the diamond in the vacuum cleaner bag was only just beginning. Soon after, Nordstrom management began spreading the tale throughout the company and the culture. The story was featured in *Loop*, the quarterly employee magazine. The company produced a video about the incident, centered on an interview with the customer. The video clip was shown to virtually all 50,000-plus Nordstrom employees, who were encouraged to "create your own version of the 'diamond story.'"

To top it off, the video was played at the company's annual share-holders' meeting in Seattle. After the clip, Erik Nordstrom told the audience, this story of customer service "raises the bar." Then he introduced Eric Wilson, Bart Garcia, and Tom Fraley, all of who were flown in from North Carolina, along with members of their families. They were greeted with a standing ovation.

"How can we create an environment where people like them can do great things?" asked Erik. "Eric Wilson didn't ask what his job description was in loss prevention. Job one for us is to take care of the customer." You can't "clerk" it at Nordstrom.

Quite often, great service has nothing to do with selling. For example, a female customer was driving past the Salem Mall in Oregon on her way home. She heard a noise from her car but kept on going. When she arrived home, she examined her car and discovered that one of her hubcaps had fallen off. She figured it happened when she was driving past the mall. She couldn't get over there right away, so she called the Nordstrom in the Salem Mall, told the operator what had happened, and asked if a store employee could venture out onto the road to see if the hubcap was there. This being Nordstrom, an employee did just that. He found the hubcap, brought it back to the store, washed it, and notified the customer, who came in to pick it up.

"We love that story," said Peter Nordstrom, executive vice president of the company and president of its full-line stores, "because it means people don't just think of Nordstrom for buying things, they think of us as a place where they can find solutions."

Consider this solution from Kristi, a telephone customer service specialist, who went above and beyond to rescue a customer in need. The customer, who was traveling in France, was out of money, her ATM card was not working, she had no place to stay and nothing to eat. Thousands of miles away from home, unable to reach her family and with no resources, the customer contacted her credit card companies, hoping they would temporarily increase her line of credit. None were willing to help her, until she contacted Nordstrom. Without hesitation, Kristi increased the customer's line of credit so that she would be able to afford food and lodging until her flight back home. The customer said that Kristi took care of her "like family."

Two employees from the Nordstrom store in Chandler Fashion Center (Arizona) truly went above and beyond for some customers on their special day. One of the salesperson's personal customers was planning a surprise wedding, full of special touches for his fiancée, in her best friend's backyard. Everything from the invitations to the photographer was falling into place— except for somebody to perform the ceremony.

As the day of the wedding drew near, the customer went to his Nordstrom salesperson to have his tuxedo fitted—and it came up in conversation that the salesperson was an ordained minister.

"Does that mean that you could marry us?" the customer asked.

The salesperson said "yes."

His department manager happily gave him the time off. The wedding was a phenomenal success, and the customer's bride was happily surprised. The salesperson held up very well under the pressure of meeting family and friends for the first time at the wedding. And the department manager, who is also an artist and owner of his own gallery, invited the happy couple to the gallery to pick out a wedding present. The couple continues to frequent the store as they live happily ever after.

Don't Judge a Customer by Her Shoes

Although it's important to pick up on what the customer is wearing, veteran Nordstrom salespeople caution that snap judgments based on a customer's appearance can cause you to lose out on a potentially lucrative sale. For example, when Patrick McCarthy was working at the Tacoma store in the 1970s, a woman in her fifties walked through the sportswear department one morning dressed in tacky clothes and a pair of old white tennis shoes with a hole in the toe. There was no stampede to wait on her. After a few minutes went by, McCarthy came over to say hello. Two hours later, she had purchased about $5,000 worth of sport coats, shirts, and, sweaters, which, she explained, were uniforms for the crew of her boat. She asked McCarthy to put all the items together for her driver to pick up. The customer turned out to be the daughter of a famous American industrialist, and she was on her way to her estate in the San Juan Islands.

"That was a tremendous learning experience," said McCarthy. "Never judge a book by its cover; open it up. If you treat a kid who is buying a $19.95 belt the same as a businessman buying a $1,995 Oxford suit, you will be successful. That kid might become a customer for life."

Inverted Pyramid

The inverted pyramid symbolizes the freedom and support inherent in a Nordstrom culture that encourages ownership and entrepreneurship. Individual front line Nordstrom salespeople essentially run their own businesses within the larger corporate structure. They are the most important elements in the organization and management supports them every step of the way. The system enables and encourages each salesperson to use his or her own personality, approach, and skills to succeed.

In the employee newsletter, *Loop*, salespeople were asked the question: "What Does the Inverted Pyramid Mean to Me?"

An employee at one of the Nordstrom Rack stores in northern California recalled the time when her store was closing for the night and all of the cash registers were shut down. Before she left, she noticed that one credit card payment had accidentally gone unprocessed. "When I saw that the payment was due that night, I drove it over to our Stonestown store, which was still open, so I could make sure the customer wouldn't receive a finance charge. Because my manager believes in me, I believe in myself and feel confident to take on more responsibility instead of doing the same job and the same tasks every day."

If she didn't have the confidence of her manager, she might have decided, "Oh, why bother. It's not my problem. Somebody will process the bill tomorrow."

Now, imagine you were that customer. You get your bill from Nordstrom and you notice that there is a late charge. You think to yourself, "Not only did I pay that bill on time, I paid it right in the store. How did Nordstrom screw this up?" Instantly, this customer has a negative feeling about Nordstrom. But that didn't happen because one empowered employee, inspired by her employer's (and her coworkers') commitment to customer service, drove miles out of her way to save that customer a late charge. At Nordstrom, small gestures count as much as grand gestures.

Return Policy

Empowering the people on the sales floor with the freedom to accept returned merchandise (even when the damage was done by the customer) is the most noticeable illustration of the Nordstrom culture because it is the one that most obviously affects the public.

Nordstrom stands behind everything it sells. The return policy is virtually an unconditional money-back guarantee. (There are some exceptions, due to public health laws, in certain departments, such as cosmetics.) If customers aren't completely satisfied with their purchase, for whatever reason, the store takes it back, no questions asked.

If a customer comes into the store with a pair of five-year-old shoes and complains that the shoes are worn out and wants her money back, a Nordstrom employee has the right to use her judgment to give the customer her money back.

This is not hyperbole. Packing for a move across the country, a Seattle woman discovered two pairs of long-forgotten, never-worn dress shoes, still in their original boxes with Nordstrom price tags and a sales slip—from 20 years earlier. Half-joking, the woman returned the shoes to Nordstrom, which reimbursed her the original price of the shoes, a total of $98.50.

Doesn't that unconditional policy invite abuse? Sure it does, but central to the Nordstrom philosophy is a desire not to punish the many for the dishonesty of a few. Which is not to say that returns are not often frustrating for Nordstrom salespeople. You have the customer who "borrows" a dress for a couple of years and then returns it. Nordstrom will put its foot down in egregious situations.

"Now, if somebody goes too far, we'll say that although fairness is our credo and that's how we try to live our retail life, this adjustment is not fair," Bruce Nordstrom wrote in his memoir. "The ones we say 'no' to are people who have a lengthy history of wearing something and then returning it."

Bruce added that Nordstrom has its liberal return policy "not because we're good guys; we do it because it works. We want to do more business. It serves our purpose to be nice to people, to wait on them, to turn the other cheek. We've always believed that the happiest customer is the one leaving the store with a shopping bag in her hand."

Top salespeople realize that returns are part of the game; they take back the returns with a smile, knowing that many of those customers will return. Some enterprising Nordstrom salespeople will even send a thank-you note to a customer who has returned a purchase. Wouldn't a gesture like that get your attention as a customer?

Such resourceful thinking was what Everett, Elmer, and Lloyd Nordstrom had in mind when they established this generous warranty back when Nordstrom was a two-store operation in the 1920s. The brothers dreaded having to deal with obviously outrageous or unreasonable returns, so, they reckoned, if they could pass off the responsibilities for the adjustments and complaints, the business would be more personally enjoyable.

"We decided to let the clerks make the adjustments, so they would be the fair-haired boys," recalled Elmer. "We told them, 'If the customer is not pleased, she can come to us and we'll give her what she wants anyway.'" Tracking the costs for the first year, they found that they could afford the return policy, which became a point of difference from its competition. In a world where most retailers make returns an ordeal, Nordstrom made the experience as painless as possible, which generated priceless word-of-mouth advertising. It still does.

Elmer's son, Jim, once said, "Returns are the best way in the world for us to own the customer forever. When somebody comes in with a return, that's the time to really separate yourself from your competition. Greet them with a big smile. With the kind of prices that we charge, if people don't feel they can return an item if something's wrong, then they aren't going to buy it.

"In the case of shoes, they may walk around forever to make sure they fit. If you take back the item with a smile and no questions asked and the customer walks out the door happy, what's that worth? That's a lot. It's the best sales closure we have as a company. What a wonderful opportunity for a salesperson to own a customer."

Perhaps the most famous Nordstrom return story (which the national press frequently cites) is the tale of the salesperson who gladly took back a set of automobile tires and gave the customer a refund. What doesn't ring true about this story? Nordstrom has never sold tires. The story sounds apocryphal.

Nevertheless, it's true. In 1975, Nordstrom acquired three stores in Alaska from the Northern Commercial Company, a full-line department store that sold many products, including tires. After Nordstrom bought the stores, the company converted them to Nordstrom and eliminated lots of departments, including the tire department. So, when the customer—who purchased the tires in that building from Northern Commercial (not Nordstrom)—brought them back to Nordstrom, the return was accepted. This has become the quintessential Nordstrom return story, and one hears variations of it all over the United States.

For years, one of those tires was hung on the wall of the stockroom as a reminder of the power of the return policy.

Empower Employees to Make Good Decisions

Even as it grows, Nordstrom strives "to put as much responsibility as possible into the hands of as many people as possible," said Bruce Nordstrom. "That's the only way to give the culture a chance to progress. Otherwise, it can't be done. With more than 50,000 employees spread out over 3,000 miles, if you were dependent on a Nordstrom family member, you couldn't do it. We keep pushing the power down to the sales floor. Human nature being what it is, there's no question that if you are in an ivory tower, sitting at a desk behind your computer and your reports, you'll say, 'I'm scared of the decisions they're going to make down on the floor.'

"I sometimes sit in my office here and wring my hands, but I know that in the long run, our way is better. I think I'm a good shoe man. I think with a little crash course, I could be a good shoe buyer today. But there's no way I should be telling these folks what colors to buy, what heel heights to buy, what patterns to buy, because I don't know enough about it. I'm not talking to those customers every day. If that confidence in the individual is repeated over and over and over again, it creates power there. This isn't a real scientific business. If we could harness people's goodwill, energy, and ideas and have it all go in one direction, then it would have to be successful."

Nordstrom has confidence in its salespeople's ability to make good choices. If the store manager or department manager isn't around to approve a key decision, the salesperson can make the decision—even if it's wrong. Such freedom attracts people who give a damn, who don't require a lot of supervision.

Van Mensah, the men's apparel salesperson at Nordstrom's Pentagon City, Virginia, store, joined the company in 1988, and he has built an extensive international clientele of gentlemen whose jobs bring them to the nation's capital. His thousands of active customers include international businessmen, government officials (particularly international diplomats), as well as U.S. senators, congressmen, and military officials.

Mensah routinely makes 25 to 30 customer calls per day. "This is where the whole philosophy of empowerment makes so much sense," he said. "You are empowered to use your own time wisely."

One day, back in 1990, Mensah received a sad letter from one of his better customers, an executive with a well-known Swedish-based manufacturer. The gentleman had recently purchased some $2,000 worth of shirts and ties from Mensah, and when he mistakenly washed the shirts in hot water, they all shrank. He was not writing to complain (he readily conceded the mistake was his), but to ask Mensah's professional advice on how he should deal with his predicament.

Mensah immediately put a telephone call through to Sweden and told the customer that he would replace those shirts with new ones at no charge. He asked the customer to mail the other shirts back to Nordstrom—at Nordstrom's expense.

This story was written up in a Nordstrom annual report to shareholders entitled "A Company of Entrepreneurs." This publicly traded corporation told its shareholders that they have an employee who gave away $2,000 worth of merchandise—and that they are so proud of him, they are featuring him in the annual report.

"I didn't have to ask for anyone's permission to do what I did for that customer," said Mensah. "Nordstrom would rather leave it up to me to decide what's best."

Most companies can't afford to give away $2,000 worth of goods. In this case it was a good business decision because of the loyalty it bred in a valuable customer. But don't be diverted by that grand gesture. Great customer service doesn't have to be the grand gesture. It can be just as powerful when it's a small gesture, a human kindness.

For example, a customer named Christine Virtue, who has a Christian ministry with her husband, Brian, posted a Nordstrom experience she had with her young daughter, Morgan, who has special needs.

"Lately I have been dealing with multiple school systems, physical therapists, occupational therapists, and doctors who all specialize in working with children and more often than not I have left more hurt, sad, frustrated, or misunderstood," she wrote. "Then I go to Nordstrom. And they of all people 'get it'?"

Morgan, who has cerebral palsy, wears a brace on her lower leg, so her parents had been forced to buy her two pairs of the same shoe two sizes apart.

At Nordstrom, the salesperson told her that she could buy the shoes that Morgan liked in the two different sizes. They would break up the pairs of shoes so that each fit the proper foot—and charge just the price of one pair. That is standard Nordstrom policy for any fitting discrepancy over a size-and-a-half.

"Literally tears sprang to my eyes as Morgan and I picked out really cute shoes that she could wear. We have been going to Nordstrom for Morgan's shoes ever since. We leave there feeling special not because of Morgan's needs, but because of the way we are treated. Nordstrom is committed to serving its customers and they demonstrate consistently an awareness of what it's like to be the customer or client. They treat us in ways that reinforce for my daughter that her brace and cerebral palsy don't have to define her and in ways that speak to me as a parent and say, 'We get it, we want to make life a little easier for you.'"

Nordstrom will even sell a customer *one* shoe. After one of his customer service presentations, Robert Spector was approached by one of the attendees (who works for a major financial services company), who was on crutches: Her left leg had been amputated from the knee down.

"I've got a Nordstrom story for you," she said. "I would go to other department stores and ask if they would sell me one shoe. They would be nervous and ill at ease, and would tell me that they could not do that. Against the rules! Finally, I went to Nordstrom and asked if they would sell me one shoe. The saleswoman said, 'Absolutely,' and they charged me half the price. I'll always give Nordstrom my business."

Let's say that she bought a $300 pair of shoes. Instead of a $300 sale, it was a $150 sale. She's told that story to untold numbers of people. Was that gesture worth $150 in advertising? Nordstrom thinks so. That's why it empowers its salespeople to do whatever it takes to satisfy the customer.

Top salespeople don't look for the one spectacular sale that will make their day. Instead, they are committed to planting the seed for an ongoing business relationship and to do what's necessary to regularly nurture that seed.

Sometimes great customer service at Nordstrom has nothing to do with making a sale that day.

For example, a customer contacted her Nordstrom salesperson in Tacoma after the customer had gotten a botched hair coloring at a salon. The salesperson called her own hair stylist and booked the customer in for an appointment the next day. "The true sign of a person who has their clients' best interests at heart is going the extra mile to help without any expected return," wrote the customer, whose letter appeared in Nordstrom's employee newsletter, *Loop*.

A manager at a Nordstrom store in the Midwest sent this letter to Nordstrom management about the compassion of Mary, a cosmetics salesperson in her store:

"A customer from Wisconsin has never been to our store and has never seen Mary's face. Mary helps her entirely by phone. From the beginning, Mary did all the right things. She suggested great products, included free samples, went to different cosmetic lines to find products, and shipped everything to Wisconsin. Mary has been following through to take care of the customer's needs for about a year.

"Sadly, the customer has cancer. A year ago she received her diagnosis and deals every day with the effects of the disease. She has had trouble feeling pretty, has lost her short-term memory and sense of smell, and worries about her husband.

"The customer says the service she receives makes a world of difference. She feels beautiful again, and says that Mary has been part of her recovery process."

After Robert Spector gave a speech in Indianapolis to a convention of tour operators, a woman came up to him and said, "I have a Nordstrom story for you, but it's too complicated to tell it to you here." Robert asked her to send him an e-mail, which, thankfully, she did.

Here is her letter:

Last Fall, I accompanied my 33-year-old sister, Cindi, to Seattle, where she was to undergo a bone marrow transplant for leukemia. If you've ever seen anyone after they've gone through one of these things, you would think they had been in a concentration camp. Skinny, no hair—not even eyebrows, pale and sickly looking. My sister had an especially hard time and ended up in a wheelchair for a few weeks due to muscle weakness.

After she was discharged from the Fred Hutchinson Cancer Institute, we stayed in Seattle for a few months to keep a constant watch on her progress. At one point, the doctor cleared Cindi to take a few "road trips" to get out of the apartment. Her favorite thing to do was go shopping, so we hauled the wheelchair and my sister to downtown Seattle and ended up in Nordstrom's. Since we are from the East Coast, we had heard of the reputation of Nordstrom's customer service but never actually visited a store. [*This story occurred before Nordstrom opened stores on the East Coast in the late 1980s.*]

Picture me wheeling around my sister, pale and sickly looking. (I forgot to mention that my sister was a model and always took pride in her appearance.) Well, most people avoided us because she looked awful! We were going through the cosmetics area of Nordstrom's when a woman from the Estée Lauder counter stepped out in front of us and asked if she could put some makeup on my sister! God love her, I don't know her name, but for a half hour, my sister felt like a million bucks. This cosmetics saleswoman knew she wouldn't make a sale because my sister looked like she was about to die, but she knew she could make a difference in my sister's last days.

My sister died shortly thereafter, but I will always remember the woman who made her feel like a beautiful human being—knowing she wouldn't make a sale, but she made a difference.

Cross-Selling

To maintain that loyal customer following, salespeople can depart from their departments to sell merchandise to their customers in any department throughout the store. Nordstrom believes that once a salesperson has established rapport and a relationship with a customer and has helped that customer put together the right look, the salesperson wants to make sure all of the customer's needs are met in order to complete the package.

When finishing up with a customer in his or her department, a salesperson who wants to do a little cross selling might ask: "Where are you going next?"

For example, you're buying a suit in the menswear department and you realize you need some shirts and underwear; your suit salesman can sell those items to you, even though they are in a different department. That salesman could even sell you a sweater for your spouse or a watch for your daughter.

A personal stylist in Southern California said, "I helped a customer who was going to Mexico City to get married. She bought a bunch of new clothes and after we were finished, I said, 'What about your husband? What's he going to wear?' She said, 'Oh yeah. Show me what you have.' I took her downstairs and she bought him a sport coat, slacks, and some cuff links. It's always important to ask about the customer's other half."

The freedom to sell throughout the store gives go-go salespeople greater opportunity for higher sales. A top saleswoman once described her business as "one-stop shopping. If it's not nailed down, I'll find it for the customer. A customer once wanted a case of hangers, so I ordered them from our distribution center. Another customer wanted to buy some of our long plastic garment bags. I don't make commission on those things, but it's part of the service I provide. I sell service; not merchandise."

A men's furnishings salesperson in Texas doesn't confine her product knowledge to men's furnishings. She needs to know the products in several departments.

"I have a lot of men that I sell everything to, including shoes," she said. "Now, I help a lot of women who are the spouses of my clients. They like the way I take care of their husbands, so they ask me to take care of them. I've expanded, especially over the last year, to take advantage of that. On my card, it says, "men's and women's wardrobe consultant." My store manager wanted me to put that on my card because I was doing such good volume in ladies."

Dump the Rules: Tear Down the Barriers to Exceptional Customer Service

When it comes to taking care of the customer, Nordstrom has only one rule for its employees: "Use good judgment in all situations." Such a simple direction makes life easier for individuals who respond to a straightforward customer service philosophy.

For some people, this corporate philosophy is thrilling and liberating. "Wow. My manager thinks I have judgment of any kind—good, bad, or indifferent—and she's going to let me exercise it." For others, being empowered to follow just a single rule is terrifying. Too much empowerment.

In the early 1990s, when Nordstrom was hiring for its new store in Pentagon City, Virginia, the company received many job applications from individuals who had worked in the military and federal bureaucracies. One former bureaucrat actually told a Nordstrom executive, "If you give me a hundred rules, I'll be the best darn employee you ever had. But one rule? I don't think so." That kind of person doesn't want freedom; he wants to be told what to do. He feels more comfortable leaving his brain at home. Unless you are looking for an automaton, don't hire that person.

"Because we don't have many rules, we don't have to worry about breaking them," a Nordstrom employee said. "We're judged on our performance, not our obedience to orders."

Jim Nordstrom, the beloved cochairman who died in 1996, hated rules because they got in the way of customer service and the Nordstrom philosophy of empowering employees. Jim felt that the more rules an organization has, the farther and farther it moves away from its customers. When that happens, the rules become the most important consideration to employees—not the customer. It's as if these unempowered employees wrap the rules around them like a security blanket, and then proclaim to the customer: "You can't hurt me. I'm protected by the rules."

Jim once said, "The minute you come up with a rule you give an employee a reason to say no to a customer. That's the reason we hate rules. We don't want to give an employee a reason—from us [management]—to say no to a customer. We feel that the majority of the people we hire want to do a good job and want to be successful. I think that's true of most companies." Jim felt that after people are hired, management at many companies do "vicious things" that turn off employees and take the fun out of people's jobs. "If you give them a hundred rules, you've taken away any empowerment that they can have."

Back in the days when Jim and his brother John N., cousin Bruce, and cousin-in-law Jack McMillan ran the company (from the late 1960s through the mid-1990s), Jim was fiercely protective of Nordstrom's free-wheeling entrepreneurial culture and was willing to fight to do whatever it took to maintain it—even if it meant challenging employee grievances over wrongful termination.

He once said, "I would rather we lost lawsuits from time to time than keep employees [who] are not up to our standards. Because a weak employee will make the others around him weak, and drag them down." With that in mind, the company tore up its rule book and told its managers, in Jim's words: "You can't rely on these rules. You can't sit back and wait for an employee to break a rule and then get rid of them. You have to sit down with them, one on one, and communicate."

At Nordstrom, customer service means treating each customer as an individual, learning the customer's likes and dislikes, and treating her as a whole person. Customer service comes from the heart. Then individual salespeople add their own personal touches, where they create a relationship in which the customer feels as if she is working with a friend, rather than just a salesperson.

When we fall short of providing good service is when we overcomplicate things. Instead of relying on using good judgment to do what's best for the customer, we get caught up in rules, policies, or procedures. Rules and policies are a company's perspective on a situation. Good judgment is using the customer's perspective.

A new employee immediately picked up on the idea that, "You learn to live in the gray area at Nordstrom," where "We might not do things exactly the same way each time. You must look at each situation with new eyes and make sure you respond to the individual needs of the issue right in front of you instead of applying a cookie-cutter solution. Living with ambiguity at Nordstrom can be challenging, but in the end it keeps our responses to people and issues very real versus acting like a big, impersonal company."

Indeed, at a Recognition Meeting, a manager praised an empowered salesperson in her department by saying, "She's not afraid to make a mistake."

Knowing they will receive full credit when things go well and full blame when they don't, real Nordies enjoy their entrepreneurial, empowered freedom. "I would never be comfortable in an environment where there are a lot of rules," said Van Mensah.

"Because we don't have too many rules," said a salesperson in the Pacific Northwest, "we don't have to worry if we're breaking them." Salespeople are judged on their performance, not their obedience to orders. This salesperson recalled the time when a customer in her department misplaced a shopping bag containing three bars of soap that had been purchased in the lingerie department. "I went over to lingerie and got three more bars of soap and gave them to her. She thanked me and said, 'I can't believe you did this.'"

The bars of soap were only 90 cents apiece, but they produced a happy customer.

5

Compensate According to Results

Competition is a key element of our culture. If done right, a commission incentive system encourages better service and team play.

—Blake Nordstrom

All the nurturing in the world can go only so far. Monetary compensation must be part of the equation. Nordstrom believes in paying people according to their achievements so that they can earn as much as their talents and efforts can generate.

Everett, Elmer, and Lloyd Nordstrom, who bought the business from their father, John W., in the late 1920s, knew that the best way to attract and retain motivated self-starters was to pay them according to their ability. Beginning in the early 1950s, when Nordstrom was selling only shoes, total employee compensation has been based on commissions on net sales.

Commission sales and bonuses "gave them added incentive to work harder, and by working harder, they were often able to build a loyal customer following," Elmer Nordstrom wrote in *A Winning Team*, the privately published family history.

Commission sales are a prime reason why Nordstrom salespeople embrace the empowerment that the company affords them. Two-thirds of employees have a variable pay component to their total compensation. That means they have the opportunity to increase their pay when they achieve results against defined targets or milestones. This philosophy of pay for performance motivates front-line people to challenge themselves and their teams to greater achievements.

The standard commission at Nordstrom is 6.75 percent on apparel sales. Commission rates vary according to product category.

Each salesperson has a designated draw, which varies with each department and is determined by dividing the hourly rate by the percentage of commission. That hourly rate varies, depending on the prevailing rate in each region.

At the end of each pay period, sales-per-hour performance is calculated by taking the gross dollar volume of items sold, subtracting returns, and dividing that figure by the number of hours worked. For example, a salesperson rings up $22,000 in sales in an 80-hour pay period. Subtract $2,000 for returns, and the net total sales are $20,000, or $250 per hour. That salesperson's commission for the pay period is 6.75 percent of $20,000, or $1,350.

Top salespeople can make in excess of $200,000 annually. The average department manager's salary is $49,500 per year, but a manager is able to earn a six-figure income depending on a number of factors including individual performance, sales volume, and whether the manager is opening a new store or supporting an existing store.

If salespeople aren't making enough in commissions to cover their draw, then Nordstrom makes up the difference between commissions earned and their hourly rate. Employees who fail to regularly exceed their draw are targeted for special coaching by their department manager. If it doesn't appear that a career in sales is for them, they are either assigned to a non-sales area or are let go.

Nordstrom's nonstop emphasis on sales creates a dynamic tension among employees, all of whom have ready access to sales figures from all departments and stores in the Nordstrom chain; they can compare their performance with that of their colleagues—whether those colleagues work across the selling floor or across the country.

One of the most important performance barometers is sales-per-hour, or SPH, in the Nordstrom mother tongue. Each employee's semimonthly sales-per-hour figures are posted clearly in a back room of the store for everyone in the department to see. Therefore, you know how I'm doing and I know how you're doing. Needless to say, the bottom of the standings is not where you want to be.

Commission Sales Versus Customer Service

Some might feel that there is a dichotomy between giving spectacular customer service and earning commission sales. It's true that, in some cases, salespeople are happy to get the immediate sale and are even happier to move on to another customer. They don't see themselves in a long-term relationship with a customer because they don't see themselves in a long-term relationship with their job.

At Nordstrom, top salespeople argue that, because their compensation is linked to satisfying the customer, it's in their best interest to act responsibly. The best Nordstrom salespeople know that if they take care of the customer, the dollars will follow.

Patrick McCarthy remembers that, when he was working with customers, "I never thought about the cash register. It will always be there."

Salespeople can't look at the customers with dollar signs in their eyes. With Nordstrom's liberal, virtually unconditional, money-back return policy, if people aren't happy with what they've purchased, they are going to bring it right back. So, just trying to make a sale for the sake of selling something is a waste of time for both the salesperson and the customer.

"A happy customer will refer me to her friends," said a Nordstrom salesperson. "She won't do that for someone she feels doesn't have her best interests at heart."

To motivate salespeople and managers, Nordstrom is constantly running sales contests. From their earliest days, the Nordstroms (all of whom are intensely interested in sports and are big boosters of the University of Washington's athletic department) initiated sales competitions to promote rivalry among salespeople. If the store was overstocked in red pumps, for example, they would have a red-pump-selling contest, with the top sales performers rewarded with cash, flowers, dinners, or trips. "In a sense, every day was a contest," Elmer Nordstrom recalled. "Everyone tried to do their best, so that they wouldn't be stuck at the bottom of the list."

Each division in the company runs monthly Make Nordstrom Special (MNS) contests, where good ideas or suggestions—for sales, systems, or other facets of the operation—are rewarded with cash. The winners are honored at the Recognition Meeting.

Over the course of the year, individual departments, stores, and regions are recognized for outstanding sales and customer service. Again, these awards—fueled by the performance and success of individuals—help to foster the importance of the team.

But these contests require constant vigilance because, as one might expect, Nordstrom's emphasis on generating high sales occasionally tempts a handful of employees to try to find ways of rigging the system or outmaneuvering their teammates.

For example, in the early 2000s, the corporate shoe department ran a one-day sales contest among all the shoe departments in all the stores in the chain. The rules were simple: $500 would be awarded to every member of the individual department that sold the most pairs of a particular brand of shoes. In addition, employees would receive $5 for each pair of that brand that they sold.

But a small number of salespeople at the downtown Seattle store manipulated the contest. They sold shoes to each other and rang up sales for coworkers, family members, friends, and customers—with full knowledge that a few days after the contest was over, the shoes would all be returned, thanks to Nordstrom's unconditional, no-questions-asked return policy. But internal security systems noted an unusually high volume of returns on the brand in question, as well as a high number of incidents of employees ringing up sales for themselves, which by itself is cause for termination. After an internal investigation, 8 of the 17 employees in the department were fired.

Despite this kind of behavior, Nordstrom's top sales performers wouldn't change the commission-oriented, goal-oriented system because competition—both external and internal—stokes their competitive fires. That wouldn't happen if they were paid only an hourly rate. Knowing that their commission reflects how hard they work instills a different kind of drive, based on what they produce.

"Healthy competition is good: We love to win," Nordstrom tells new hires in its company literature. "If you thrive in a high-energy, competitive team environment, you'll love it here."

Finding the right balance between rewarding individual achievement, as well as teamwork and customer service, is the key to success.

Goal Setting

For all the people involved in sales, recognition comes from achieving goals. Goal setting binds every level of the Nordstrom organization. Salespeople, buyers, and managers are perpetually striving to meet personal, departmental, store, and regional goals for the day, month, and year, and to surpass what they did during the same period a year ago. If a department fails to achieve one day's goal, the manager raises the following day's goal.

Peer pressure and personal commitment push the most competitive employees toward constantly higher goals. Work shifts often start with a reminder of the day's goals; managers regularly quiz salespeople on their individual goals. A store manager (who earns bonuses based on sales increases and expense goals as a percentage of sales) might rally the troops by getting on the public address system, before the store opens, to tell a story about someone who just sold $1,000 worth of cosmetics to one customer.

The company encourages a creative tension among its salespeople, who have ready access to sales figures from all departments and stores in the Nordstrom chain, so they can compare their performance with that of their colleagues across the selling floor or across the country.

Every top Nordstrom salesperson is goal-oriented. Literally all of these stellar performers feed off the recognition they receive from their customers and from Nordstrom. Reaching their goals motivates them. The best of the best always set ambitious goals for themselves, and when they meet those goals they continue to set the bar higher and higher—and work harder and harder to sell more and more year after year.

A Seattle shoe salesman describes himself as "totally goal-oriented," and said that those targets keep him "focused." He always carries a notebook with him, "so that I know what sales I recorded on this day last year. I can trace it back four years to see whether or not I'm growing. Every day, when I walk into the store, I look at the figures I wrote yesterday. Setting a goal only sets the process in motion because goals are constantly changing."

Without goals, said a junior sportswear buyer in Portland, Oregon, "you don't have a direction and you lose perspective on why you are there." On the other hand, she cautioned, "If you take a goal too seriously, it will ruin the fun of achieving it. Half the challenge of the goal is making it. And when you do make it, you pat yourself on the back. And if you don't make it, you say, 'Next time, I'm going to try a little harder.'"

Top Performers

The company compensates those who reach specific sales volume goals with additional commission, stock, and other perks. Because it's given out quarterly instead of yearly, this reward is put within reach of new salespeople. The company found that offering newcomers an obtainable goal makes starting with Nordstrom a better experience. Every rookie needs a little success.

The top-performing salespeople at Nordstrom achieve the designation of Pacesetter. Pacesetter used to be decided by meeting or surpassing a predetermined annual goal of sales volume. But, over the years, the company has tweaked the plan, to make it more easily accessible for newly hired employees and part-timers. The company now uses a sales-per-hour goal to better recognize all top-performing salespeople.

Every year, Nordstrom raises the target goal figures, depending on how many people achieved Pacesetter the year before. Generally, 8 to 12 percent of the salespeople in each division make Pacesetter.

Pacesetters are given a personalized certificate of merit, business cards, and note cards emblazoned with the Pacesetter designation, and a 33 percent store discount credit card (13 percent more than the regular employee discount) for one year, and cash, which varies, depending upon how many years the individual achieved Pacesetter status.

After 10 years with the company, Pacesetters receive a Nordstrom stock award, which varies depending upon how many years they have achieved Pacesetter status. Employees who achieve this status 15 or more times during their career and have at least 15 Retiree Discount years of service, regardless of their age, receive a 33 percent discount through the remainder of their employment and throughout their lifetime.

In 2010, there were 2,416 Nordstrom Pacesetters. Several dozen surpassed $1 million in sales volume for the Pacesetter year; a small handful has done better than $2 million.

Each year, Pacesetters and other Top Sellers and their guests are treated to a little rest and relaxation as a thank-you for all their hard work. For example, they might be given an all-expenses-paid trip to

Las Vegas or Miami Beach that includes a reception and dinner hosted by the Nordstrom family.

Becoming a Pacesetter takes dedication, hard work, and a feeling of ownership of their own business, which comes about through empowerment.

"When you have star salespeople, they ought to get paid like stars because they earn it," said Bruce Nordstrom.

Loyalty and Ownership

The Nordstrom family has always considered employee loyalty something to be earned, not expected. Because brothers Everett, Elmer, and Lloyd felt that the commitment to loyalty started with them, they wanted to provide an opportunity for their employees to make more money than any other retail salespeople.

"Some companies demand loyalty from personnel, but we felt that loyalty should come from us to them, first," said Elmer.

Nordstrom's employee profit-sharing retirement plan inspires motivation and encourages loyalty. The company wanted to make it easy to retire for people who had done a great job. The program began in 1952 because the brothers wanted to make sure their employees would have money for retirement beyond Social Security, and they wanted to help the company attract better personnel.

"It was a natural development that reflected our basic philosophy: The better we treated our people, the better our people performed," recalled Elmer.

Today, with employment in most industries in such a state of flux, the only way people will be loyal to a company is if they are given appreciation, respect, good pay, and a piece of the action. Nordstrom feels that even people who don't make it a career with the company can benefit from working there.

Peter Nordstrom recalled the time he was asked to discuss career choices with a young woman starting out in the business world.

"I told her that even if you don't know exactly what you want to do, Nordstrom is a good place to work because if you can come here and understand what it's like to interact with customers and do that well, then this experience is going to benefit you in some way. It's going to look good on your resume if you spent some time here and did well. Every company has a customer orientation to it. We're fortunate to be known for that. So use that to your advantage. Learn something here. Do the best you can at it, and let it take you where it takes you."

As of April 2011, 6,536 employees had been with Nordstrom for 11 to 20 years; 1,890 for more than 20 years.

6

Communication and Teamwork

We're All in the Customer Service Department

If you're not a team player, you won't have a long career at Nordstrom.

—Bruce Nordstrom

Nordstrom demands individual achievement and unselfish team-work, both of which are essential to (a) the culture, (b) the experience, and (c) the bottom line.

In fact, teamwork may be the more important of the two. You can be the highest grossing salesperson in the organization, but if you don't give service to your fellow employees, you will not survive. Consequently, a Nordstrom employee must be a team player who makes a contribution to the success of his or her department, store, region, and company, particularly in team selling competitions and contests, which are essential motivating tools to the Nordstrom Way.

Nordstrom constantly reinforces the idea that when the company is at its best, it is the result of a group effort. Nordstrom is both a collection of individuals and a seamless team, with each member of that team expected to be ready, willing, and able to take care of each other, while taking care of the customer.

For example: The manager of a women's wear department in a Nordstrom store in the Pacific Northwest wrote a letter, which appeared in the company newsletter, *Loop*, about the teamwork of one of her salespeople.

> "I was apprehensive about leaving my crew for a vacation because of the heavy shipments of anniversary merchandise we were receiving. Tom must have known I was nervous about being gone. He offered to swap shifts with a coworker over the weekend so he would be at the opening. This would allow him more time to work the merchandise,

set the floor, and pull figures. I was impressed with his confidence as he read my expectations and said, 'No problem!' And before I left, he showed initiative by calling me with a suggestion for organizing the stockroom. His ideas saved everyone else a lot of time and energy!"

"When I returned, the stockroom looked great; there was a pile of figures on my desk for my review; and the jeans were all sized and folded on the back wall. Tom showed great leadership in stepping up to get things done, and he also effectively delegated projects to other crew members. I feel fortunate to have such an amazing person on our floor."

Communication

Regardless of the industry, most companies are horrid at internal communication, which they often cite as their biggest challenge.

You can't have teamwork without communication. You can't have communication without teamwork. And without teamwork and communication you can't inspire and empower employees to take ownership.

To achieve these goals, Nordstrom begins with an open-door policy, where managers and executives are always available to converse with each other by any and every means necessary. (The quarterly employee newsletter used to be called *Open Door*.) The company communicates with all 50,000-plus employees in a variety of directions and channels—corporately, regionally, locally; within stores, within divisions, within departments, and so on, using e-mail, company intranet, blogs, and other technology, including the good old telephone. To have true internal communication, an organization must use all channels, just as it uses all channels to communicate with external customers.

Leaders must be in close contact with their teams to avoid uncertainty and misinterpretation. Whenever there is an announcement of a major change in the business or an important new initiative, the company's strategy is for the information to "trickle up" the inverted pyramid in face-to-face meetings. Regional managers are responsible for communicating information to their store manager teams; store managers are responsible for relaying the messages to their department manager teams; department managers are responsible for passing the information on to those at the front lines. The simple idea is to keep everyone abreast of what's going on.

Nordstrom sends out monthly and quarterly e-mails announcing sales results, recognizing individual and team achievements, and alerting people to upcoming special events and new initiatives. At the annual State of the Company employee meeting, management talks about past results and future goals.

Using internal "connect boards," employees can anonymously submit questions, suggestions, or concerns. It could be a question about the temperature of fitting rooms or about how the commission system is structured. Usually within 24 hours, the appropriate person or team will follow up with an answer. Through this system, store managers get to hear what's on the minds of their team members and then have the opportunity to respond. This forthright communication strengthens the connection between salespeople and support groups and builds the sense of the whole store as a team.

Loop, the employee newsletter, is the primary company-wide communication tool. Published four times a year, *Loop* is mailed to the homes of employees at all levels and also is posted on the company's intranet site. The publication keeps employees connected through articles on the shared culture and common purpose of driving results and improving customer service, as well as general company news, philanthropic efforts, customer service letters, fashion trends, selling-related features, and company-wide employee recognition.

In Person

Even with all the electronic channels of communication, Nordstrom believes that there's no better channel than face-to-face. The company conducts periodic regional Town Hall Meetings where employees have personal interactions with members of the Nordstrom family and other offices and managers.

Sometimes those interactions involve sharing tough news. For example, when Nordstrom decided to close its store at Circle Centre in downtown Indianapolis, Erik Nordstrom traveled there to tell the employees before the news was made public.

Every day, before each store opens, the store manager conducts morning announcements over the intercom system so that everyone can hear the information while they prepare their departments for opening. The store manager provides a review of the prior day's business, highlights individuals who exemplified outstanding service, recognizes employees who had great results (such as the top 10 individual selling performances), reads customer service letters, discusses new product in the stores, gives an update on store events, and motivates employees for the day by establishing sales goals.

Sometimes, these morning announcements morph into rallies, when everyone in the store gathers together in a particular location to have face-to-face meetings and conversations on a variety of topics, such as building customer relationships, details on new merchandise or an upcoming event, such as the anniversary sale, held in July, which is the largest volume-driving event.

The anniversary sale is not about price reductions on items from the current or past season, but rather price reductions on the next season's (fall/winter) merchandise. Nordstrom places that merchandise on sale for a 30-day period. After that, it is marked back up to regular price. Many retailers across the country have copied this idea.

Nordstrom picked up the idea of having a preseason anniversary sale featuring new (rather than end-of-season) merchandise. "Best's had started it in order to provide business for the slowest time of the year, which was in the month of July," recalled Bruce Nordstrom. "They bought some special-purchase fall items. We thought it was a good idea, but we thought it would be an even better idea to bring in the best stuff. We did that, and it really made the difference."

Every store in the company holds an anniversary rally, where managers and salespeople showcase sale merchandise, share goals, and announce competitions and contests. Buyers work with vendors before the sale. Planning meetings and product seminars are held and extra employees are hired. To get everyone excited, many fun events are planned around this special time.

Nordstrom stores close early the night before the sale to prepare. All employees, even corporate and non-selling employees, pitch in to get ready for the sale. When the store opens early the next morning, employees share healthy snacks and coffee. Corporate and regional leaders sell, stock, and greet customers on the first day of the event. When the sale is over, there are multiple awards given for top performances among stores, regions, and merchant teams.

All of Nordstrom's sales are presold. Customers who spend over a certain amount and/or have a Nordstrom credit card are given a preview of the items that will be on sale. Shortly before the sale, customers can choose what they want, give their credit or debit card number, and have the items held for them until the day the sale begins. On the first day of the sale, the items are charged to their card at the sale price. The customer doesn't have to worry about items selling out.

Teamwork and Competition

When it comes to building positive team relationships, employees are expected to know, understand, and support team goals, and to cooperate with—and show respect for—their coworkers throughout the company.

For example, every year, the President's Cup is awarded to the full-line stores that rack up the largest increase in comparable sales over the previous year. The competition is divided into three categories, depending on the size and sales volume of the stores. The categories are named after founder John W.'s three sons: Everett, Elmer, and Lloyd. One of the three current Nordstrom brothers—Blake, Peter, or Erik—makes an appearance in the winning store, and presents the store employees with a cash prize of as much as $100,000. A President's Cup is also awarded to the new (open two to five years) stores that have the highest sales increases in their category. The Rack stores have their own competition in three categories, based on sales volume, named for Bruce, John N., and Jim of the third generation.

What does it take to win the President's Cup? In an interview in *Loop*, Teresa Burgess, who was then store manager of Short Pump Town Center in Richmond, Virginia, said "Our key to winning the President's Cup was to stay focused on giving customers an exceptional experience and building relationships. We coached 'relationship selling' by getting our people to think big. The key is to look beyond the customer standing in front of you and think, 'What can I do to make his or her life easier?' Maybe they need clothes for the kids, or have an anniversary or a relative's birthday coming up. Everybody is short on time. How can we make their life easier? That was our rallying cry, 'Just make it easy.'"

Just make it easy. It should be the rallying cry for every company.

What Does Teamwork Look Like?

"Our success hinges on the support of other salespeople and management and support staff," said a Nordstrom department manager. "You have to be grateful on a consistent basis for your entire team."

Teamwork takes many forms at Nordstrom. Sometimes it's subtle, other times it's obvious.

A customer wrote a letter to the company to commend the special service she had received on a visit to the Nordstrom store at the Mall of America in Bloomington, Minnesota. It wasn't just any day; it was her wedding day. The customer had forgotten to pack a few items and her maid of honor had yet to buy her dress. The two women had rushed to take the hotel shuttle to the mall and had about an hour before they would have to return in order to get to the church on time.

The bride and maid of honor were greeted by a salesperson (whom we'll call Lynn) in the Mall of America store, who was apprised of the situation and the time constraints involved. Lynn picked out the perfect dress for the maid of honor, and then handed off the soon-to-be-bride and her maid of honor to a shoe salesperson.

While the two customers were trying on shoes, the original salesperson brought over earrings to complement the dress. They purchased two pairs. Putting the proverbial cherry on top of the cake, Lynn asked the store concierge to find the name and location of a mall merchant from whom the customers could buy silk flowers. That is what teamwork looks like.

Of course, the two salespeople in this story both earned commission money on those sales. But sometimes the most impressive examples of teamwork occur when salespeople don't earn a commission, when they selflessly go out of their way for the greater good of their department or their store or their region or their company—or just because it makes them feel good.

For example, Bob Bullard, a million-dollar salesperson in the menswear department at the Corte Madera store in California, was the subject of a story written by a coworker:

"Bob is a true team player who gives A+ customer service to his clients, his coworkers' customers, and all of us who work in the store. He is always smiling, knows his merchandise, and helps educate our customers, and us, too. He jumps right in and cheerfully helps when someone from our team looks 'confused' about an upcoming appointment. Bob never assumes that he should receive part of the commission for helping—and he does so much.

"Recently a couple called on a Saturday afternoon. The wife needed an outfit for a wedding that they were going to attend. I called to get her information, and she asked if we could also help fit her husband for a suit. She mentioned that he had recently become partially disabled and was in a wheelchair.

"When the couple arrived, all of the sizes I had pulled for the husband were wrong because his disabilities were more extensive than I had understood. Not certain how to handle the situation, I called Bob and he immediately came up with someone from the tailor shop. He knew how to fit the customer's very narrow shoulders while still making the trousers work. Bob spoke with the gentleman and understood his challenges. He made him comfortable and sold him two suits with all the accessories. The wife bought her outfit from me, and the two of us had $5,600 in sales.

"But the best part was Bob's dedication to making sure everything was right for the couple. The wife had tears of joy in her eyes when they left."

This is a perfect example of the company's striving to strike a balance of customer service, teamwork, and individual achievement. The two Nordstrom employees gave the husband and wife a positive customer service experience, they worked well together, and they each made a sale: win, win, win.

Teamwork Across Departments, Business Units, and Geography

Creating—and sustaining—relationships with and between other departments is crucial. Without that relationship, how can one part of your business appreciate the role that another department plays in the success of the company? Nordstrom believes that teamwork brings individuals closer together and fosters greater understanding. The company urges departments within stores to work with each other for the greater good.

"I really encourage my crew to create relationships with different departments," said the cosmetics manager at a California store. "Think of all the different customers they have access to that we don't share and vice versa. We try to include as many departments in our promotions as possible."

If a Nordstrom salesperson can't find a particular item in her store, she will do a merchandise check for her customer to find the item at another Nordstrom store, whether it's down the road or across the country.

"When a salesperson from another store calls, I'll ask, 'How can I make your day?' They love it," said a salesperson who understands the concept of teamwork.

When one employee conveys that kind of positive feeling of cooperation and teamwork, your organization will be well on its way to giving customer service the Nordstrom Way.

In this era of multichannel service—where organizations can do business with their customers either through their brick-and-mortar operations, website, mail, or telephone—companies are learning how best to coordinate these individual business units.

Nordstrom Direct, which has one fulfillment center in Cedar Rapids, Iowa, handles customer orders from the company's mail-order catalogs and website. The Nordstrom Direct distribution facility is set up differently from those of the full-line stores (the large Nordstrom stores, as opposed to the smaller Nordstrom Rack discount stores), because each business unit has its own considerations and requirements. But they also, at times, must work together.

Nordstrom Direct partners with full-line stores to provide a seamless customer experience. As one employee noted, "The best thing about this relationship is that neither party looks at it as 'Well, it's your customer or it's my customer.' It's always *our* customers. "

Nordstrom understands the challenges of fulfilling these orders for store teams. In an article in *Loop*, management argued that, "When something is a win for the customer, it's a win for our business. It may not always feel that way, but we think it's safe to say that when we put the customer first, we derive more value out of the subject of enhancing our service reputation than any advertising campaign or promotion could possibly create."

Customer Service Behind the Scenes

We tend to think of customer service as the direct interaction between front-line employees and customers. But what are the roles of support staff that have little or no direct contact with customers? Support staff, like all Nordstrom employees, look at the Nordstrom experience from the customer's perspective. What does the customer see? What does the customer want in that moment? This is where teamwork comes in.

At most organizations, support people see no connection, no cause and effect, between what they do and how they impact the customer experience. When they view their jobs through a narrow prism, they don't feel compelled to take ownership.

It is an article of faith at Nordstrom that support people have a profound impact on customer service because if they don't do their jobs, then front-line people can't provide the best customer service experience.

Providing seamless service is a total team effort, whether it's the personal shopper in Cedar Rapids who chats with the customer online to help her find the perfect item, or the support employee at the full-line store who finds that item in stock and hands it off to logistics to get it out to the customer, or the salesperson who locates an out-of-stock size for a customer by using the online store, or the Nordie at the distribution center who picks the order from the shelves and makes sure it's shipped out on the truck.

So how do you get back-office or support people—employees who rarely, if ever, deal with a customer—to understand how the team works?

Because Nordstrom believes in praise and recognition, the company is ingenious at finding creative ways to honor and single out non-sales personnel, whom Blake Nordstrom called, "the unsung heroes of our business."

For example, the White Glove Contest, a Nordstrom tradition for decades, gives cash rewards and honors to the housekeeping/maintenance departments that keep their stores clean and inviting to the customers. As management points out in the company newsletter, "A store can't win this award unless everyone is involved."

"Whether it's a clean bathroom, a quickly fulfilled Direct-to-Customer order, or a rush alteration on the perfect dress for an event tomorrow night, if it makes a difference to the customer, it makes a difference to our company's service reputation," said a store manager. "Each and every one of us can impact the experience a customer has when shopping at Nordstrom."

Here's an example of how non-salespeople seized the opportunity to provide great customer service. This story was by the store administrator at a Nordstrom store in the Southeast, who wrote about two employees in Loss Prevention. Let's call them Josh and Sam.

"These two men are awesome! I know I can always count on them. Last weekend I was expecting a shipment from FedEx that did not arrive on time. I told Josh, and he took the initiative to call FedEx and make arrangements to pick the shipment up at the local station, which happened to be close to where his coworker, Sam, lived. Josh called Sam and asked him to pick up the shipment before he got in at 7:00 A.M. on Monday. Sam arrived with just one box that was smaller than I expected. Apparently, there were supposed to be three boxes. He returned to the FedEx station to retrieve the remaining boxes without question. Thank you, gentlemen, for taking care of the store and me!"

Tailoring to the Customer

The Tailor Shop and the Alterations department are vital parts of the selling team. Those men and women are not faceless functionaries; their names and pictures are posted prominently in the fitting areas.

A department manager at a Nordstrom store in New Jersey sent in this heroic tale that recognizes the talents of several employees in the Tailor Shop and Alterations department:

"I had a customer who was leaving for Milan the next day. He only wanted a pair of Norsport pants to wear between business meetings. He mentioned that he needed other things, but was going to buy them there because he didn't think it would be possible to get the alterations done in time. I showed him a lot of things that he might like for his trip—why waste time shopping for clothes on your vacation? We tried to find pants with exact length sizes, but to no avail. I called a tailor from the Tailor Shop. He graciously agreed to have them done in an hour.

"Then the customer needed a jacket. I showed him the washable suede from Newport Harbor. Both he and his wife loved it, but the sleeves had to be shortened. The Tailor Shop was overwhelmed, so I asked Alterations for help. One employee offered to have it done first thing in the morning. The customer was happy to pick it up on the way to the airport. The employee in Alterations asked if someone from the Tailor Shop could just measure the sleeves. One of the tailors who came down to measure them agreed to be a hero and do the sleeves before the customer came back for his pants, rather than having Alterations take care of it in the morning.

"Three of the customer's shirts also had to be pressed for the trip. I thought I had done enough to bother the guys in the Tailor Shop for the rest of the year, so I proceeded to press them myself. One of the tailors was just finishing pressing some other items, so I asked him to show me how to work the big steamer. He proceeded to do the shirts for me, and wouldn't stop even when I asked him to.

"I let the employee in Alterations know that I appreciated her help, but that the Tailor Shop came through and everything was ready for the customer when he returned. He was so pleased, and what was originally a $39.50 sale turned into a $650 sale! Please recognize everyone—they each deserve a special prize for this heroic."

A salesperson from the Short Hills Mall store in New Jersey sent this letter to Blake Nordstrom, to recognize the lengths her team members went to on her behalf to make sure they did not disappoint a customer.

"One crazy Saturday in October, we had a call from a customer who was supposed to receive a Roberto Cavalli dress overnight for Saturday delivery. She was wearing it to an event that evening and the dress never arrived due to DHL's mistake. The customer was upset, as she had purchased shoes and accessories to go with the dress. Anne from the Collectors department, Bob (the store manager), and I sprang into action to try to alleviate this issue for the customer. We went to competitors to see if they possibly had the dress in stock, but no such luck. To make matters worse, it was the last dress of its kind in the collection.

"The customer mentioned to the Collectors' salesperson that there was another dress in a boutique in Northern New Jersey (about an hour from the store) that was her second choice to wear to the event, but it needed alterations. The customer said that she had to leave for her event in two hours and there was no way that she would have time to pick it up and have it altered within two hours.

"That is when the Short Hills team went into action. Bob flew out the door to go to the store in northern New Jersey to buy the

$2,000 dress for the customer. He then met us at the customer's house. Tanya, the Alterations manager, agreed to go to the customer's house to do the alterations. Then Anne and I drove with the Alterations manager to the customer's house with several dresses in tow, just in case the one from the boutique did not work.

"We all converged on the customer's house—the store manager with gown in hand, the Alterations manager with her needle, and the salesperson with her amazing fashion sense to dress the customer head to toe. Then Tanya pinned the gown in the customer's bedroom and then hand stitched the hem of the dress at the kitchen counter! We all had such a sense of urgency for this customer and truly wanted her to feel good about what she was wearing to the event.

"If that were not enough, the customer's sister was visiting her. The sister was not pleased with her own outfit that she was wearing to the event that night. She tried on one of the gowns that Anne had brought along and ended up purchasing a $2,500 Dolce & Gabbana gown to wear to the event and a $2,500 suit that she just had to have as well!

"I was so proud to watch such excellent customer service in action. This is what our company was founded on."

Impressing the Boss

Robert Spector will take a little credit for this story, which happened after he gave his keynote presentation on Nordstrom in Orlando, Florida, to a leadership meeting of a Fortune 500 company. A woman in the audience, who was new to the company, wrote this letter to Blake Nordstrom and the manager of the Nordstrom store in Orlando:

"I have been shopping at Nordstrom for years, but I wouldn't say I was a loyalist until today. After hearing all of the stories on how employees had gone over and beyond for their customers, I thought to myself, 'I must buy some shoes this weekend when I get back to home in California.'

"At one of the breaks, the logistic team announced we would be attending a team outing that night at Universal Studios. Please dress casually. Oh Nooo! I don't even have a pair of jeans with me. They didn't tell us to bring casual clothes. I only have yoga gear for my room. I can't walk around and ride roller coasters in heels. I quickly remembered what Robert had told us and I gave Nordstrom a call.

"I first tried the Nordstrom Rack because it was closest. The rep said they didn't do personal deliveries, but she spent the time checking. She told me to contact the main store because they have personal shoppers. I've never used a personal shopper, so I thought, this must be $1,000, but I'm in a bind, so I have to at least check it out. I called and told the operator that I heard about the excellent customer service and that I needed to be outfitted by the time the shuttle bus departs for the outing at 7:30 P.M. She quickly directed me to the manager of Personal Shopping. I explained my dilemma. My salesperson, Martinette, literally had 10 minutes to speak with me during my break. She asked all the right questions. Body type, shoe size, style, age, type of event.

"I explained this was the first time I had met my CEO and CFO and I need to be casual, comfortable, but still stylish and professional. I asked her, 'How does this work? Do you bring a selection to the hotel? Can you come to the hotel?' She said, 'I will text you at the number you are calling from and I will send photos of the items. You can text me back. Once we have a match, we will bill you and send everything to the hotel.'

"Fifteen minutes later, she pulled two outfits—one sweater with jeans, and another spunky top with jeans. Totally stylish!!! Then she found three pairs of sneakers for me in varied colors to match! I cannot believe how easy it was. She said, 'We are boxing it up. We need to leave now to make sure you get it in time.' Sure enough, it arrived and fit perfectly. I AM SOOOOO IMPRESSED! YOU HAVE A LOYAL customer for life. I will be stylish during my corporate outing and will walk with pride and ease.

"One final note: I know marketing and I have a big mouth and a strong network. I will tell EVERYONE about this wonderful experience. Thank you, Martinette and thank you, Nordstrom!!!"

When your organization can communicate to every member of your team that you have a unified purpose—to satisfy the customer—then you have taken a major step toward becoming the Nordstrom of your industry.

7

Citizen Nordstrom

Doing Well, Doing Good

We like to start off on the right foot, to give back something to the community before we open our doors.

—Bruce Nordstrom

Corporate social responsibility has become a new benchmark for customer loyalty. A significant portion of today's consumers want to spend their money with companies that they believe are also good corporate citizens.

While Nordstrom is in the business of consuming, the company wants its customers, employees, vendors, and shareholders to understand that it is also in the business of doing good, while doing well.

Nordstrom has had a long-running dialogue with its employees and customers to learn what matters most to them when it comes to being a good citizen, and it has created a comprehensive strategy of social responsibility based on the input of a task force of leaders from all areas of the company.

The task force focuses on four key areas "pillars," in the company's jargon. These areas are: caring for employees (including health and wellness initiatives); supporting the communities in which the company does business; protecting human rights (in countries where the products that Nordstrom sells are made); and being good stewards of the environment by developing inventive programs around recycling, packaging, sustainability, and other green concerns.

As we have said previously, Nordstrom believes that the best ideas for improving the company's performance come not from management but from front-line employees. To that end, the company solicits green or cost-saving suggestions from employees, and encourages them to share their ideas with whoever is in charge of that particular initiative. The men and women who come up with a good idea to create positive change are designated as "Nordstrom Cares Heroes."

One such hero was Julie Dieringer, the store administrator in downtown Portland, who read an article about how a Nordstrom vendor, Columbia Sportswear, was reusing its boxes. She sent an e-mail to the Nordstrom family, along with a link to a video on Columbia Sportswear's website that demonstrated how the program operated. "I see how many boxes get recycled," Julie wrote in her e-mail. "Then they put things in brand-new boxes. Why not just reuse some of the good boxes?" Soon afterward, Julie heard back from the family saying they were going to implement her idea. The company established criteria for determining which boxes should be reused: Are they structurally sound (no rips or tears)? Are they covered with too many logos?

The shoe business generates a lot of paper content that eventually find its way into the waste stream. That's what prompted Tacey Powers, a divisional merchandise manager for women's shoes, to suggest that Nordstrom partner with a footwear company, UGG Australia, to reduce the amount of excess material inside each UGG shoe box.

After her idea was vetted by Nordstrom's Corporate Social Responsibility team, it was presented to UGG Australia, which is the only two-time recipient of the Nordstrom Partners in Excellence Award. UGG responded by putting into effect several changes in product packaging, including removing a surplus piece of cardboard that separated each individual pair of shoes or boots, and replacing tissue paper used to stuff boots with a recyclable, post-consumer-waste insert. To protect the product, they also added a biodegradable shoe bag. As a result of these changes, about 44,000 pounds of paper waste were saved in the first two months alone.

"Nordstrom Cares"

Visitors to Nordstrom.com can link to "Nordstrom Cares," where the company details its progress and procedures on all of its corporate responsibility initiatives. When it comes to self-evaluation, Nordstrom is disarmingly honest. They will tell you whether they're making progress or not doing enough. For example, under its "Recycling Goals for 2010," Nordstrom aimed for "Reducing total waste sent to landfills and/or incinerators by recycling plastic, glass, metal, paper, corrugated cardboard, and organic waste."

Adjacent to the column that spelled out this goal is another column headed "2010 Results." Nordstrom gave itself an evaluation of "Made Progress But Below Target: We didn't meet the higher goal we set in this area but we still had strong results, which we attribute to our successful nationwide recycling program. Our Fulfillment and Distribution Centers each had a 98 percent waste diversion rate, and our Rack stores had an 83 percent rate. Though 41 percent of our stores participated in composting programs to recycle organic waste from our restaurants and specialty coffee bars, we faced challenges with the organic waste/recycling infrastructures in certain markets where our locations exist."

In the next column, "2011 Focus," the company said: "We'll hold ourselves to a high goal for waste diversion again in 2011. We see opportunity for improvement in recycling rates at our full-line stores, in new store and remodeling construction, and in our corporate facilities. We're already seeing progress related to the organic waste challenges we've faced in certain municipalities and hope to achieve an increase in this area next year."

There is a similar evaluation of the progress in energy, transportation, paper and packaging, water, natural and organic food offerings, human rights, and safer cleaning products.

In this day and age, where disinformation can be easily discovered, Nordstrom believes that honesty is more important than sophistry.

Recycle, Repackage, Reuse

According to Nordstrom, the most frequently asked questions from both employees and customers concern the company's commitment to using recycled materials, supporting eco-friendly products, and offering responsible choices to its customers.

All gift boxes and shopping bags are made from 100 percent recycled content. "If it came from us, you can put it in the recycle bin," Nordstrom assures its customers.

Shopping bags from Nordstrom Rack are made of 80 percent recycled content, and they have an additive that helps them decompose in landfills in the event that they don't make it into a recycle bin.

All catalogs, annual reports, and paper-based employee communications are made with Forest Stewardship Council certified stock with 30 percent post-consumer waste. Most Nordstrom gift cards are made of 50 percent preconsumer/postindustrial recycled PVC stock. All inks are soy-based.

The company's distribution and fulfillment centers reuse corrugated shipping boxes when possible to help cut down on the amount of packaging. These centers can sell almost everything—from hangers to plastics to wood pallets—back to the recyclers.

The distribution facility for Nordstrom Direct (web and catalog sales) established a single-stream waste process that reduces landfill waste and converts what was formerly waste into usable energy that is transferred back to the power grid.

A new shipping capability allows Nordstrom to consolidate orders in order to reduce the number of individual packages showing up at one time on a customer's doorstep.

In its stores and office buildings, Nordstrom labels all recycling containers and displays educational messaging in the hallways, meeting rooms, and near the cash wraps, and spreads the word through awareness fairs, manager meetings, and e-mails.

The restaurant division recycles all cups and napkins, and all to-go bags and containers are recyclable. All brewed ice tea is organic, and all eggs are from cage-free hens. Organic matter is being recycled in many stores, where municipality or third-party programs make it viable.

From an energy standpoint, Nordstrom continues to reduce usage per square foot. New spotlight technology and efficient fixtures with automatic controls have reduced electrical consumption in both the front and back of the house.

Nordstrom wants to show its customers that fashion and the environment can coexist.

In 2010, Nordstrom took an abundant material—the plastic water bottle—and converted it into a stylish, versatile tote bag, made from 100 percent post-consumer-recycled material. Approximately 10 16-oz. water bottles go into the making of each bag—material that otherwise could be headed for landfills. The bag looks modern and feels strong, stands up to rain, snow, sun, and sand, and can be washed and wiped clean. It also folds up into its own compact pouch, so it fits inside the customer's regular handbag. When fully expanded, the bag is big enough to hold two shoe boxes. Each tote features an earth-friendly illustration by artist Ruben Toledo.

Supplier Diversity

To reflect the communities where it does business, Nordstrom has an aggressive Minority- and Women-Owned Supplier Diversity Program, which it began in 1989, to attract qualified businesses to consider Nordstrom as a potential client.

When Nordstrom enters a new market, the company sets out to cultivate minority-owned and women-owned vendors of office supplies, food, music, photography, and other services, including construction. Through this program, Nordstrom encourages these vendors to supply locally produced merchandise. Thanks to the company's decentralized buying, Nordstrom is able to bring in these smaller vendors and test their products. Since beginning the program, Nordstrom has purchased more than $9 billion in goods and services from minority- and/or women-owned vendors.

This program helps form community contacts with a wide range of business and civic leaders, and it gives an opportunity to boost the economic vitality of the communities.

Contributing to Communities

During the course of a year, the company and its employees support hundreds of community organizations through contributions, outreach programs, special events, and volunteering their time.

When Nordstrom opens a full-line store in a new market, it's a big deal. The key is to come in "with all guns blazing," said Bruce Nordstrom. "I think we get off to a running start better than anybody. We say 'Let's be beautiful, let's be great, let's have a beautiful opening party, and donate lots of money to local charity.' We haven't made a cent yet, but we're going to do those things first."

Just prior to a grand opening, Nordstrom partners with several local nonprofits for a gala event, such as a formal celebration, a fashion show/benefit, or kids' tile painting parties with all proceeds going to those nonprofits.

For example, when Nordstrom opened its first Cincinnati store in Kenwood Towne Centre in 2010, a sold-out gala raised $165,000 to benefit three nonprofits in that community: the Cincinnati and

Queen City chapters of *Links, Inc.,* a global organization committed to enriching, sustaining, and ensuring the cultural and economic survival of all people of African origins; the Chris Collinsworth ProScan Fund, which promotes breast cancer awareness and education; and Lighthouse Youth Services, which advocates for abused and neglected children and for families in crisis.

Prior to the 2011 opening of the store in Newark, Delaware, at Christiana Mall, the company hosted a preopening gala for 1,600 people, which raised $123,030 for the Delaware Art Museum; Nemours/ Alfred I. duPont Hospital for Children; and the Wilmington Chapter of Links, Inc.

Also in 2011, Nordstrom took a completely different philanthropic tack by opening an experimental store in New York City, where all the profits were committed to children's charities. The two-floor, 11,000-square-foot store called Treasure & Bond, in the Soho neighborhood, gives no evidence that it is owned by Nordstrom. With concrete floors, open ductwork, and reclaimed furniture and fixtures (from Nordstrom full-line stores), Treasure & Bond has an intentionally unfinished look. Nordstrom changes which charities it donates to every three months. The recipients in this store's first year included the New York Public Library's programs for youths and The Edible Schoolyard NYC.

EXPERIENCE

*We are a theme park of retailing in a sense. We are about food, fashion, and fun.
The whole point of everything we do is to make the customer happy for the long haul.
You have a good experience and you want to do it again. If people are satisfied and excited
about the experience of shopping at Nordstrom, they will come back. And if we haven't
created that atmosphere, they won't come back. It's just that simple*

—David Lindsey, vice president of store planning

8

Create an Inviting Place

Brick-and-Mortar Still Matters

Everything we do is to enhance and romance the merchandise. We work to create a special place that feels inviting, warm, and comfortable.

—David Lindsey, vice president of store planning

Having launched more than 100 full-line stores in every corner of the United States, Nordstrom has perfected an opening day plan of attack that has the precision of U.S. forces invading Normandy on D-Day.

As we saw in Chapter 3, Nordstrom empowers veteran employees to open stores in new markets. Seeing how the Nordstrom Way travels is a tremendous growing and learning experience for all employees—both old-timers and rookies.

Opening day is the culmination of months of preparation by hundreds of employees, who for the first time are working together as a team. As the day draws closer, they meet both as department teams and the total store team, with every one of their colleagues. They hear directly from their store manager and members of the Nordstrom family, who attend every opening.

The final rally before the doors open is visibly emotional as the team focuses on their collective achievement—getting the store ready for customers. The store manager offers words of inspiration and thanks for being part of the opening team. Each department within the store is recognized for its contributions. The rally is fun and upbeat—many of the departments bring signs and props, and they cheer, applaud, and sometimes perform dances or skits when their department is mentioned.

A Nordstrom store opening always gets wide coverage from local news outlets. "It is the day women across the city have been waiting for," gushed the beautifully coifed and tailored Houston TV news anchorwoman. "Friday marks the opening of Houston's first Nordstrom store at the Galleria Mall."

Cut to an attractive 30-something African-American woman: "We are so glad they finally came to Houston. It's going to be fabulous. The store is so great. The customer service is fabulous. We look forward to having Nordstrom in Houston."

The scene shifts to a local TV newscast, a few months later, this one in Austin, Texas. "It's the moment Austin shoppers have been waiting for," said the bespectacled anchorman, a slight smile creasing his face. "It was a madhouse today at Barton Creek Mall."

Cut to a 40-something blonde shopper: "There's no place else I would rather be. I've been countin' this down for about six months," she drawls. "We're going to be in there all day. I don't plan on leaving the store."

Cut to a shot of thousands of pumped-up women (and a smattering of men) outside the new Nordstrom store, waiting patiently (some impatiently) for the doors to open for the first time, shouting "Nordstrom! Nordstrom! Nordstrom!" as if they were cheering for the University of Texas Longhorns football team.

Meanwhile, at the entrance to the store, a big brown roll-down grated door momentarily separates the customers from the sales staff. Excitement is building on both sides of the 30-foot-wide divider. It's hard to tell who is more eager—the shoppers or the salespeople. Finally, at precisely 9:30 A.M., the barrier slowly inches upward like a giant garage door. Hyperkinetic shoppers in front of the throng hardly wait for the divider to rise up all the way. They duck underneath and begin dashing into the store in a scene reminiscent of the running of the bulls at Pamplona. Some are dancing, some are skipping, some with feet barely touching the marble floor beneath them—they are being high-fived by beaming Nordstrom employees, who have lined up at the entrance to applaud and cheer the new shoppers—a long-standing company tradition.

"Fabulous styles, wonderful service. I've become a part of it in California and I just can't quit," enthuses an ecstatic longtime customer, who proudly holds up a T-shirt featuring a picture of her holding her car license plate in a holder that proclaims: "I'd rather be shopping at Nordstrom." One of the highlights for her on that day was when she got Blake, Peter, and Erik Nordstrom to autograph her T-shirt.

It's the same in Charlotte, Richmond, Boca Raton, Pittsburgh, Las Vegas, even on Michigan Avenue in Chicago, which is one of the world's greatest retail venues.

When Nordstrom opened a store in Cincinnati's Kenwood Town Centre, a group of women arrived at 5 A.M. As Nordstrom employees filed in before the opening, they noticed several women already set up in the parking lot as if for a tailgate party at a football game. The backs of their cars were open and tables were set up with candelabras, mimosas, and pastries to celebrate their first Nordstrom experience.

There is nothing quite like the opening of a new Nordstrom store to quicken the pulse and open the purse of serious shoppers. This, you might say, is the "Nordstrom effect"—the way you set the stage for creating an inviting place for your customers.

What's Inside

What's inside the store—the residential feeling, layout, design, lighting, seating, wide aisles, large fitting rooms, display fixtures, amenities, and, of course, the merchandise—is an essential facet of customer service the Nordstrom way.

Convenience and openness are the trademarks of its store design, Nordstrom wants to make it as easy as possible for customers to circulate and shop throughout the entire store, and for salespeople to help them do just that.

Nordstrom wants customers to be able to meander through the store without impediments such as narrow aisles. When a customer is walking down an aisle, and another customer is coming the other way, there must be enough room for both to comfortably pass each other. If a customer feels crowded or that her space is violated, she may decide to leave—and not buy that sweater or running shoe or Chanel handbag.

The waiting areas around elevators are extra wide to make it easy for customers to navigate with baby strollers or wheelchairs, and the elevators themselves are larger than average, making it easier to load and unload those strollers and wheelchairs.

"When they think about our store, customers don't think of jostling and banging, they think of a pleasant experience," said retired cochairman John N. Nordstrom (grandson of the founder). "What's that worth?"

Store layouts typically resemble a wheel. The hub of the wheel is the escalator well; the spokes are the marbled aisles that lead directly back to each of the 30 or so departments. The subtleties and details create a shopping experience that is easy, convenient, and pleasurable.

Most department stores in suburban malls have just one elevator; Nordstrom has two elevators in its three-level stores. In Nordstrom's two-level stores, there is one elevator, but that one is larger than elevators found in other department stores. Escalators are 42 inches wide, compared with the 32-inch-wide escalators found in most department stores. This enables couples, parents, or children to ride side by side.

Unobstructed sight lines enable the customers riding on the escalators to quickly scrutinize the full spectrum of the selling floor they are approaching. The aisles give shoppers the freedom to circle the store and to plunge into the center of each individual department. Nordstrom believes that if you can lure customers to the perimeter back walls of the store, they are more apt to make a purchase. Unlike large retailers who close off their departments with walls or dividers, Nordstrom features departments that are freestanding. These departments are defined by lighted curtains, secondary aisles, upholstered lounge seating, custom-designed hardwood, bronze, and glass showcases, and furnishings and display fixtures that are built low, so as not to obscure shoppers' views of other departments or salespeople's views of customers.

Spaces in virtually every department are made warm and comfortable by the furnishings, as well as plants, plush carpeting, lighting, wainscoting, and artwork.

The merchandise is presented in succinct, compelling visual displays that Nordstrom describes as "aspirational"—that is, merchandise that customers aspire to buy. The displays change regularly to maintain interest among frequent shoppers.

Secondary aisles that run through the back of the departments are about 10 feet from the back wall. Along the back walls, the merchandise is highlighted and romanced, like artwork in a gallery, by spot lighting and warm wall coverings instead of paint. Every square foot is important. Nordstrom averages close to $400 in sales per square foot.

True to its heritage as a shoe store, Nordstrom's footwear departments (most stores have four or five separate ones) are its showplaces. Women's shoes are always located near the most prominent store entrance. Because shoes are the most important customer draw (after all, most people have a hard time finding a pair that fits), the company devotes about three times more space to its women's shoe department than its competitors do and fills that space with more inventory than any other store offers.

Each day, each footwear department designates a particular shoe style as the hot "item of the day," giving it greater emphasis among the sales force. Inventories of the item of the day are stockpiled just inside the stockroom door so that they are readily available to salespeople, who can receive extra bonuses for selling those featured items.

Complimentary gift boxes are available with every purchase at every sales counter.

Let's Get Comfortable

At newer Nordstrom stores, a good portion of the footwear inventory in each department is stocked directly behind that department, which makes a transaction easier and less time-consuming for both the salesperson and the customer. The other half of the footwear inventory is stocked in mezzanines, which are directly above the shoe stock, adjacent to the sales floor. With so much of the stockroom merchandise nearby, salespeople don't have to hustle up and down stairs all day; they can get in and out of the shoe stockroom in a couple of minutes.

Because Nordstrom carries so many shoes, and because most feet are tough to fit, customers are going to be in the footwear department for a while, so Nordstrom makes those folks comfortable in a homey parlor setting, with plushy upholstered sofas and chairs, custom-made to Nordstrom's specifications, The chair's legs and armrests are a bit taller and longer than average, and seating is firmer, which makes it easier for a person to stand up. Customers need to focus only on how the shoe feels. Nordstrom wants the customer to think only about those shoes—and perhaps buying another pair or two.

Not surprisingly, customers frequently comment on how comfortable the seating is throughout the store; husbands and boyfriends can be found sitting restfully, waiting for their ladies, rather than trying to hurry them out of the store. Customers will stay a little longer and try on one more shoe if they—and their gentlemen—are comfortable.

A Seattle writer named J. Glenn Evans, who penned this poem entitled "A Place to Rest," summed up Nordstrom's consideration for customer comfort:

> I followed my wife while she shopped
> From store to store she went
> I the great man was spent
> The flesh pulled on my bones like two bags of cement
> At last I found a chair
> Heaven only could have been more fair
> Of all the stores, Nordstrom was best
> They gave a husband a place to rest.

When your customers are writing love poems to you, you know you are doing a pretty good job.

An in-store piano player—a Nordstrom signature—engages a customer's senses and creates the ambiance of an inviting place. Usually located by the escalator, the Nordstrom piano has become something of a cultural icon. Condoleezza Rice, Secretary of State under President George W. Bush (and a trained classical pianist) once joked that her ability was just good enough to get her a job playing at Nordstrom. In the novel *Sleeping with Schubert*, by Bonnie Marson, the heroine (a neophyte musician) suddenly channels the classical composer when she spontaneously begins to play a piano at a Nordstrom store, setting off a series of events that eventually lead to her giving a recital at Lincoln Center in New York.

Leonard Lauder, retired chairman and chief executive officer of Estée Lauder, once commented that, "A Nordstrom piano doesn't take up much room. It's a small idea, but it's a genius idea."

Alas, Nordstrom is gradually phasing out the live piano player, which some consider a relic from a bygone era. Today's younger customers expect to hear music a little closer to their tastes.

Shopping at Nordstrom is all about the experience. Fun, of course, takes lots of forms. Like finding a hot fashion item at Nordstrom and tweeting about it to your friends. Or getting together on a shopping trip with a few girlfriends, partaking of lunch or an espresso, and taking advantage of the girlfriend dressing rooms that Nordstrom has created, where a half dozen friends can try on clothes comfortably and share their shopping experience. They might be high school girls shopping for back to school, or their moms all buying outfits for a special event. At Nordstrom, they are taken care of from head to toe—shoes, handbags, and all the accessories.

The large, carpeted dressing rooms, fitting rooms, and customer lounges are furnished with upholstered chairs and/or sofas. Fitting rooms in the more fashionable ready-to-wear departments include tables, table lamps, and telephones.

Particular attention is given to the lighting of the mirrors in the dressing rooms so that the customer can see the actual colors of the item being purchased.

Nordstrom adjusts the coolness of the dressing rooms with a dedicated thermostat that is separate from the thermostats that control the temperature on the sales floor and in the adjoining rooms. Although independent thermostats add to costs, they also add to the customers' comfort. When a customer is sequestered in a small, hot, and stuffy room, trying clothes on and then taking them off, that customer will invariably want to get through the experience as quickly as possible. Nordstrom keeps those rooms comfortable because Nordstrom doesn't want customers to leave; Nordstrom wants customers to stay. Consequently, the company will do whatever it takes to keep that customer in the store and continue to give him or her the opportunity to make purchases.

Nordstrom Innovation Lab

Nordstrom's Innovation Lab is devoted to enhancing the customer experience. Nordstrom considers the lab a lean start-up within a Fortune 500 company.

A group of young, energetic, tech-savvy employees work on software applications to make life easier for the customer. For example, over the course of a week, they came up with an application for an iPad to help customers buy the perfect pair of sunglasses. Rather than sequestering themselves in their offices, the Innovation team worked at the sunglasses department in the downtown Seattle flagship store, gathering feedback from customers on the best features for the app. Imagine: Asking customers what they wanted. Customers were able to take pictures of themselves wearing different pairs of glasses and were able to compare them side by side. Nordstrom was able to enhance the customer experience with the help of the customer. Could it be any simpler?

Why does Nordstrom make this effort? A member of the Innovation Lab put it simply: "Instead of competitors coming up with the new, fast, cool idea, we should be doing it ourselves."

Food for Thought

Another way to keep people in the store is to feed them. Nordstrom's food and restaurant services generate profits, enhance the shopping experience and, of course, give customers another reason not to leave the store.

Nordstrom has several in-store restaurant concepts, depending on the size and location of the individual store. Classic Café, Marketplace Café, and Café Bistro offer freshly prepared soups, salads, sandwiches, pasta dishes, pizza, desserts, and a full children's menu and coloring sheets to keep the little shoppers occupied.

Nordstrom Grill is an elegant, full-service restaurant located within select Nordstrom stores, with a more ambitious menu than the cafés, as well as beer, wine, and mixed drinks. All menus are developed regionally in order to cater to local palates.

Nordstrom also has a Specialty Coffee group, which consists of three different concepts that are often located outside the store or directly next to a store entrance—Espresso Bar, Ebar, and in-house Café & Coffee Bar, depending on store size and location. Each concept serves high-quality coffee and non-coffee beverages, sandwiches, salads, and pastries to Nordstrom customers as well as people walking through the mall.

The company recently added a new restaurant concept called Sixth & Pine (named after the cross streets of the downtown Seattle flagship store), which Nordstrom describes as "great comfort food with a contemporary twist—a diner with the heart of a deli, offering a range of options, from potato latkes to panko-crusted shrimp."

Something Extra

In larger stores, Nordstrom offers a concierge desk where shoppers can receive special attention, whether it is helpful information about the store, a restaurant recommendation, or assistance in calling a cab. Need to check your coat, umbrella, and packages with the concierge? No problem.

The Customer Service department in each store offers check-cashing privileges for Nordstrom cardholders, immediate posting of payments to Nordstrom accounts, answers to inquiries regarding those accounts, monthly statements, credit line increases, complimentary gift wrapping, and purchase of gift certificates.

Some of the larger stores have a SPA Nordstrom, which offers natural aromatherapy, herbal body wraps, massage therapy, manicures, and aromatic facials. Inexpensive shoe shines are available in the men's area of nearly all Nordstrom stores.

At this point, you may be saying to yourself, "My business isn't set up for a concierge service and herbal body wraps." It doesn't have to be. But is your business set up for clean restrooms?

Several years ago, two female reporters from the *Washington Post* surveyed the ladies' restrooms in all the department stores in the Washington, DC, area. Their criteria were all the things customers look for in a good restroom—ample space and supplies, cleanliness, diaper-changing facilities, and so on. Nordstrom was rated number one.

We don't usually associate clean restrooms with customer service, but why not? When your restrooms are clean and well supplied, you are telling your customer that you care about every aspect of their experience with your company.

Because parents with children also require more room, the dressing rooms and lounges (both men's and women's) are large enough to accommodate strollers and diaper-changing tables. Nearly all stores have special rooms for nursing mothers, and newer stores incorporate "family" bathrooms where a parent can accompany his or her child of the opposite sex. Some Nordstrom stores equip their children's areas with toys, coloring tables, television sets, video games, and built-in helium containers for blowing up balloons.

"We love Nordstrom because of how it makes us feel . . . accessible and welcoming," wrote a Southern California shopper on her blog. "The layouts of most Nordstrom stores are open, uncrowded, and the decor is generally warm and clean. Wonderful touches that tell me, the shopper, that someone thought about me when creating the spaces."

All full-line stores have Wi-Fi connectivity, which provides the foundation for many customer-facing tools, such as mobile point-of-sale devices (Mobile POS), which make it easier and more efficient to locate items and check prices for customers, whether in their individual store or within the Nordstrom inventory system.

These Internet-connected devices also enable salespeople to scan an item, complete a credit-card sales transaction, and produce a receipt, either electronically or on paper, without requiring customers to wait in line for a cash register. This speeds up the checkout process.

To become even more efficient, Nordstrom employees are using a variety of other portable electronic devices, such as smartphones, laptops, handhelds, and media tablets. These tools contribute to making the store a gateway to the entire retail supply chain rather than the final destination.

Selection

Nordstrom is committed to stocking its stores with a wide selection of merchandise—a combination of world-renowned brands and Nordstrom's own brands. The company operates on the premise that the more selection it offers, the less likely a customer will walk out of the store without making a purchase—or two or three.

Back in the days when cofounders John W. Nordstrom and Carl F. Wallin—both neophytes in the footwear business—ran the fledgling enterprise, "The store was so small and looked so poor that the fellows from the better factories back East wouldn't even call on us to sell us shoes," John W. told the *Seattle Post-Intelligencer* in a 1961 interview commemorating the store's 60th anniversary.

Because Nordstrom continues to want to attract people of all shapes and sizes, the company remains committed to carrying more sizes—particularly in footwear—than any comparable retailer. Unlike much of the competition, the store carries many half sizes, which help to ensure a better fit. When a customer has more than a size-and-a-half difference between foot sizes, it is policy to split sizes so that the customer doesn't have to buy two full pair of shoes.

After they have measured the customers' feet, Nordstrom salespeople are trained to show customers several shoe options. For someone with hard-to-fit feet, Nordstrom likes its salespeople to come out of the back room with as many as 8 or 10 or 12 pairs of shoes. For the customer—who has probably had difficulty finding shoes that fit him or her—seeing a salesperson loaded with all of those shoes is a remarkable experience. That's why Nordstrom maintains its extensive inventories in a range of sizes and widths.

For example, consider this story:

A man who was involved in sales for a scientific supply company wrote the store manager of the Nordstrom store at the Old Orchard Shopping Center in Skokie, Illinois, about a great customer service experience that he wanted to share. The man had an unusual size, 6½ EE, and had been having major problems finding a pair of black wingtip shoes in downtown Chicago. At a specialty shoe store downtown near his home, the salesman happily sold him a pair of Florsheim wingtips for $97 and assured the customer that the shoes were the right size. The customer had tried them on hurriedly and bought them. But when he put them on the following day, he immediately sensed that they were not feeling right, and no wonder—they were actually size 7!

"I returned them and informed the store of the mistake and asked if I could get a wingtip in my size," the customer later recalled. "The salesclerk said they didn't stock my size and it would be a special order at an additional cost. I said I don't have the time to wait and would like to return them for a refund on my credit card. The store manager refused the refund and gave me store credit instead. I asked him how could I get store credit if they don't have a shoe in my size? What would I do, buy $97 in socks? So I left angry."

After two days of shopping in countless shoe stores, the man came to the unhappy realization that no one in the city of Chicago carried his size—and if they did it would take two weeks to special order the shoes.

Finally, a friend told him about Nordstrom's extensive shoe department, so he drove out to suburban Skokie, where an outstanding salesman measured the man's feet and came back from the stockroom with six pairs of black wingtips that fit perfectly, and fully explained the benefits of each type.

"I was elated," wrote the customer, who told the Nordstrom salesman about the crummy treatment he had received at a competitor's store in Chicago. The Nordstrom salesman called the competitor's store and asked them to refund the customer's money.

Imagine getting a call from Nordstrom questioning you on your customer service? What else could the salesman from the other store do but give the customer a full refund? The customer ended up buying two pairs of shoes that day. The Nordstrom salesman now tells this story to all new manufacturers' reps that he trains. "I emphasize how total customer satisfaction means not just *the sale* but *repeat sales*!"

That kind of service is why Nordies are nurtured.

The Right Choices at the Right Time

Jim Nordstrom once said, "There's nothing more demoralizing for a salesperson than to not be able to satisfy the customer. Our number-one responsibility to our salespeople is to have the products that the customers want when the customers come into the store. You can have all the pep rallies in the world, but the best motivation is stocking the right item in the right size at the right price."

Bob Middlemas, a longtime executive vice president, learned that lesson early in his career, when he was a buyer of men's tailored clothing in Nordstrom's Oregon region. When Middlemas's merchandise manager was on sick leave, Bob filled in for several weeks. "One day, I'm sitting at my desk and I get a phone call from John [N.] Nordstrom (Jim's brother). That got my attention," Middlemas recalled. "He said, 'Bob, I was out visiting your region [in] the last few days. I went to the

160

men's furnishings department of your Clackamas Town Center store [outside of Portland, Oregon] and I noticed that you didn't have any 17½ [neck], 35-inch [sleeve] white shirts. And your tall-men's tie selection looks very, very weak, considering what a trend that is in our men's furnishings business right now. Check on that and get back to me?'"

Middlemas immediately got on the case. After making some inquiries, he came up with a clear, simple answer to the question posed to him by the man every employee calls "Mr. John": The distribution center was out of size 17½, 35-inch white shirts, but a new delivery was expected in a couple of weeks. The neckwear manufacturer said that the tall-men's ties were on their way to the distribution center and would be in the stores in a few days. The young Middlemas, eager to please his boss, felt proud of himself, "because I thought I had done my job. I called Mr. John back and said, 'I got the answers you were looking for,' and proceeded to tell him about the inventory that was on its way to the distribution center."

But Middlemas did not receive the response he was expecting. In fact, his explanation was met with stony silence on the other end of the telephone line. Finally, Mr. John replied: "Bob, you didn't understand my question. I didn't ask you where they were. I asked you why we didn't have them." The point, Middlemas realized, "was that I should figure out a way to solve the problem. If we don't have the stock, we should get it from one of our vendors so we don't walk [lose] a customer on a thirty-five-dollar dress shirt. Because if we walk him on the dress shirt, we're not going to sell him the shoes or the tie or the belt, and he's going to be disappointed in our company."

This kind of attitude and philosophy are ingrained in the Nordstrom culture. Forty years before Mr. John taught Bob Middlemas a valuable lesson, John's uncle, Everett, did something similar for one of his shoe buyers. When Everett asked the buyer why a size 7B in a certain style was not in stock, the buyer replied that it was on order. Everett asked for a copy of the order sheet. He folded it up, put it in a shoe box, and placed the box on a shelf in the stockroom. "Now," he told the buyer, "when the customer for that size 7B comes into the store, tell her to try that order on."

Nordstrom Rack

The company offers a different experience with Nordstrom Rack clearance stores, which sell Nordstrom's usual name brands at 30 to 70 percent discounts. Nordstrom sends five deliveries of fresh new merchandise a week to the Rack, which keeps bargain hunters coming back for their prey.

Unlike the full-line-store customer, The Rack customer is not interested in paying full price. Nevertheless, Racks have a profound positive impact on sales at nearby full-line stores. For example, when a Rack opened in Chicago on Michigan Avenue and recorded $600,000 in sales on its opening day, the full-line store down the street saw a 16 percent increase in sales during that same day.

Racks generate a total of approximately $1.5 billion in sales. Nordstrom projects that will double by 2015. The number of Racks is growing faster than the full-line stores, as these stores are easier to build with much shorter lead times. A typical Rack store does approximately $500 to $550 per square foot in sales in locations approximately 35,000 square feet in size, in comparison to other off-price retailers who do approximately $200 per square foot.

These stores are generally located in strip malls. While lease terms are around 10 years, Nordstrom can easily move a store to a new location if they believe results will improve. The company gets great real estate deals because Rack serves as an anchor to these shopping centers and brings customers to the area.

As the Rack division continues to grow, so do the opportunities. Rack offers a first-time employment opportunity at Nordstrom and is a developing ground in which department managers, store managers, and other key positions can grow as leaders.

A Nordstrom general merchandise manager said, "The number-one thing I learned at the Rack is that the best ideas come from the floor. That's something I practice to this day as I get out in the stores and listen to our people. It makes a big difference in your business."

That's how you create an inviting place.

9

Touchpoints

Multichannel Customer Service

When a customer shops with us, they don't see a difference between a Nordstrom store or nordstrom.com. To them, it's just Nordstrom, and they want a service experience that lives up to their expectations. We have been working to make shopping easier for our customers by breaking down the barriers between our stores, our website, and our catalogs.

—Blake and Jamie Nordstrom

In 2002, after the first Internet bubble had burst, Robert Spector's book, entitled *Anytime, Anywhere: How the Best Bricks-and-Clicks Businesses Deliver Seamless Service to Their Customers*, was published.

The premise of the book was that proven brick-and-mortar companies boasted some significant advantages over pure-play Internet competitors—with one major exception (see Spector's book, *Amazon.com: Get Big Fast*). Those advantages included a mature infrastructure, established customer base, and access to capital.

Nordstrom was one of the companies profiled in *Anytime, Anywhere*, along with fellow Seattle retailer Recreational Equipment, Inc. (REI), Wells Fargo, FedEx, and Geek Squad, which at the time was still a small, independent company before it was acquired by Best Buy.

Back then the Nordstrom Website and Direct Sales division (including mail order catalogs) was under the direction of Dan Nordstrom, second cousin of Blake, Peter, and Erik. (Today, Dan is president and owner of Outdoor Research, a Seattle-based company that makes outdoor gear and equipment.)

As early as 1993, Nordstrom, like many other retailers, was experimenting with alternative selling channels such as interactive television, which was being touted by many as the latest "new thing." That technology was designed to enable the customer to communicate directly with an on-screen Nordstrom salesperson (personal shopper) through a voice-activated conferencing system, which was a two-way audio/one-way video, so that the personal shopper didn't invade the privacy of the customer. The customer, who addressed the TV screen to trigger options, could examine the merchandise from several angles and ask the personal shopper (seen in an on-screen window insert) about size, color, and so on. Once the customer made her decision, she used an on-screen menu to select method of payment and shipment.

Around that time, Nordstrom joined with Bloomingdale's in a closed circuit home shopping show, originating from the Mall of America in Bloomington, Minnesota, where both were anchor stores. Nordstrom was underwhelmed by the results of the initial experience.

Another experiment was e-mail shopping through a service called Nordstrom Personal Touch America, a collaboration with long-distance phone carrier MCI Communications Corporation and Connect Soft, a software communications company.

None of those initiatives went anywhere.

Then in July 1995 Amazon.com was launched and the retail world was changed forever. Customer service oriented websites such as Amazon.com understood that they were not just selling things; they were involved in transactions, which lead to other transactions. That's why their sites are inviting in every sense of the word.

Dan Nordstrom identified the "tipping point" in terms of apparel on the Internet as the holiday season of 1997, when the Gap and other retailers had recorded meaningful online sales volume. In time for the next year's holiday shopping season, Nordstrom launched its website on October 1, 1998. It was a modest beginning—essentially an extension of its catalog business online, with 30,000 stock-keeping units and no special artwork.

Nordstrom's first major effort was focused on building on its roots in footwear by establishing "The World's Largest Shoe Store"—NORDSTROMshoes.com, which was officially launched in November 1999. The site offered more than two million pairs of shoes, and almost 400,000 stock-keeping units of apparel and shoes for men, women, and children.

In hindsight, Dan Nordstrom said that among Nordstrom's early mistakes was creating a footwear website that was separate from the company's main website, with a different user interface and different presentation metaphors. It was confusing for the customers. The footwear site was later fully integrated into Nordstrom.com.

Unlike many other major retailers, such as Target, Walmart, and Barnes & Noble, Nordstrom created its own website in-house. Target farmed out its Internet business to Amazon.com (as did Borders Books and Toys "R" Us). Walmart set up walmart.com in Silicon Valley, a continent away from its headquarters in Bentonville, Arkansas. Barnes & Noble's website was a completely separate business. If a customer bought a book online at bn.com and tried to return it to a B&N store, he couldn't do it because they were separate business entities with separate inventories.

In August 2000, Nordstrom.com launched more than 18 new online boutiques of name brand fashion merchandise, which was one of the most extensive selections on the web. As the years have gone by, the company's Internet channel has become more ambitious and sophisticated, and is almost as customer friendly as its stores.

A Multichannel World

The *Anytime, Anywhere* promise has been fulfilled far beyond what was believed possible at the beginning of the twenty-first century.

Today's customers can shop at virtually any store, from any place, at any time, using a wide variety of tools. They are empowered with product information, recommendations, ratings, and price comparisons. Whether the shopping experience is in the store, online, or on the phone, they want a service experience that lives up to their expectations. They demand customer service that is integrated across all channels. Customers choose the channel in which they want to shop.

And the retailers that do the best job of being there for them are the ones who are going to reap the rewards.

The website is the crucial component of a multichannel customer service strategy.

One-third of all new Nordstrom customers come through its website. The way customers use its website influences how Nordstrom shapes its multichannel strategy, which is an important tool for acquiring—and keeping—customers. Nearly one-third of Nordstrom's sales come from multichannel shoppers, who like to go online and also visit the stores. The company wants to continue to increase the number of people who shop at Nordstrom through more than one channel, because those customers spend four times as much as a one-channel shopper spends, according to the company.

Nordstrom continues to simplify web navigation in order to help customers and salespeople quickly narrow their search by using multiple criteria: category, brand, color, price point, and size. The customer can see what's available across the company's entire inventory assortment in real time because everything is updated automatically. The goal is to make shopping easier by breaking down the barriers between the stores, the website, and the catalogs.

Nordstrom offers customers free standard shipping and returns for online purchases of every size. The company previously offered free shipping for online purchases above $200 or through special promotional offers. The free shipping policy applies to Nordstrom.com orders shipped within the United States, regardless of the amount or size of the orders.

The company launched international service in 2009. Shoppers can shop the site using the currency of their choice, ship to any of several dozen countries, and pay in a wide variety of different currencies.

Single View of Inventory

Back when it was a much smaller company, Nordstrom had a decentralized, regional, sometimes freewheeling approach to buying merchandise. Even empowered salespeople could call up a manufacturer to special order an item for a customer. Nordstrom was famous for its wide and deep inventories—lots of merchandise in lots of sizes and colors.

If a store was out of a particular shoe, a motivated salesman got on the phone and called other locations to try to track down the item. "That was charming in the '80s," said Erik Nordstrom. It was less charming once consumers could easily find it online.

Today, Nordstrom's buying has become much more centralized; its inventory flow has been consolidated and modernized. Essentially all of the stores serve as warehouses for the online business.

In order to do this, Nordstrom had to change its historical way of doing business. Decentralized buyers used to replenish their own inventory and were accountable for their own results. To make the new system work, regional buyers and managers had to relinquish some autonomy to technology that ultimately would benefit the customers.

Nordstrom wanted to make sure that the same merchandise available at stores was also available online, including the latest fashions and hot new items. Online customers can now see all size and color options, and they have telephone access to salespeople.

Online and in-store salespeople have a single view of inventory in other stores and in the shipping centers, either through their in-store terminals or mobile point-of-sale devices. Not only does everyone share one single electronic view of the chain's entire inventory, each salesperson has direct access to all of it in order to get it quickly to the customer.

If a customer wants an item in another size or color, or if the item is not at the particular store where the customer is shopping, her salesperson can access the corporate-wide inventory, which makes it possible to fulfill orders online from any store if the fulfillment center is out of that item.

Nordstrom uses store networks and distribution hubs to ship online orders quickly to buyers nearby. Inventory management software helps increase efficiency by using online orders to keep excess inventory from building up in stores.

Displaying stock from both the web and the company's stores all at once was unusual in the retailing world. The end result of adding this feature was taking better care of customers and selling them more merchandise because a larger selection was available online.

If Nordstrom.com did not have the item someone wanted, it was not as if the customer would have to wait for the company to restock it. Jamie Nordstrom (brother of Dan Nordstrom) said, "If we don't have it, you're going to go back to Google and say, 'Who else has it?' We have 115 full-line stores out there—chances are one of them has it."

Order Online/Pick Up at Store

Nordstrom offers the convenience of Internet shopping along with the specialized customer service that has been a hallmark of the company. The company gives customers a full menu of shopping options, whether online or in the store.

The number-one question received at Nordstrom's call center is: "I'm looking at this item online. Can I find it at my local Nordstrom store?'"

Customers can order online and pick up the merchandise at a store the same day, thus avoiding the wait and cost of shipping. This change has increased same-store sales at stores that have been open for more than a year, which is a crucial measure in retail.

All the changes are about satisfying customers, but that translates into profits. "We can sell more without having to buy more inventory," said Jamie Nordstrom. "That plays through to margins and, ultimately, earnings."

The merchandise moves in and out of the stores much faster and more efficiently, which is crucial for a retailer like Nordstrom. Thanks to improvements in its inventory management, Nordstrom requires considerably less storage space in its brick-and-mortar stores.

Create a Customer Community

In the multichannel world, community comes in many forms. Whether in the stores or online, Nordstrom creates a community that finds fun in shopping. To build a community, you must have communication. Nordstrom wants customers to be able to connect—and share comments—with the company as a whole, with individual salespeople, with other customers, and with their friends.

The "Conversation" section of the home page is a forum for customer feedback from e-mails and other correspondence with the Contact Center, plus comments from focus groups. Customers have access to exclusive content such as a "Style Forum," where readers can solicit fashion advice from "Miss Nordstrom," a fashion expert. The page also features videos and photos from Nordstrom shoppers who offer style tips or show clothes they have bought for work or a special occasion.

After a customer purchases a Nordstrom product, he or she can go back to the product page and rate it on a scale of one to five. Customers can also create a free-form review to go into more detail on style or fit, or indicate whether they would recommend the product to a friend. Once a review is posted, other customers will be able to rate whether or not they find that review helpful. Hundreds of thousands of product reviews appear on Nordstrom.com.

Nordstrom expanded its Internet presence with the purchase of online retailer HauteLook Inc. for about $270 million in stock.

HauteLook sells luxury clothes at a discount, in limited-time online sales for shoppers who sign up as members. Started when design houses needed to get rid of unsold merchandise during the recession that began in 2007, this business model, called "flash sales," enabled the design houses to maintain their brand image. Flash sales generate quick excitement for shoppers to grab a bargain.

Social Media

Today, no self-respecting retailer with its hand on the pulse of the public would not use some form of social media to connect with customers. Nordstrom has encouraged its salespeople to communicate with their customers via e-mail, text messages, Twitter, or Facebook, and make comments in other forums such as Yelp. "Whichever approach your customer prefers, that's the best way to do it," Nordstrom tells its employees.

Using the website and customer input and feedback from its Facebook and Twitter pages, Nordstrom can fine-tune its offerings, from both a story and a product standpoint. Nordstrom passes those customer comments on to the people responsible for making decisions and responding to the customer. Salespeople use Twitter and Facebook to reach out to new customers and develop a closer relationship with current ones. They send out messages and photos to their followers to let them know about exclusive items in the store or upcoming events, and they share their expertise, advice, and recommendations.

One customer from Vancouver, British Columbia, was planning a weekend shopping trip to the Nordstrom store in Bellevue Square, across Lake Washington from Seattle. After tweeting back and forth, the store manager set her up with a salesperson who helped her find a dress in the store that she had seen online. Customers can also share their favorite items from Nordstrom's big anniversary sale. Nordstrom

Rack's global Facebook and Twitter pages provide a forum for customers to comment on things they like about the Rack or would like to see more of, such as more of a certain brand, or a Nordstrom Rack in an area where one does not exist.

Nordstrom is taking a leap of faith in empowering employees to represent the company in a sales capacity. "Use good judgment"— Nordstrom's one rule—still applies to the use of social media. The company believes that social media work best when they empower employees to use their best judgment without restricting them with rules and regulations about what they should or shouldn't say or do. Nordstrom suggests some topics to avoid, but it encourages employees to have fun and to build on their relationships with customers and each other. Social media guidelines are shared with all employees who participate and are posted for the public to view at the company website.

Nordstrom expects employees to be positive, respectful, considerate and inclusive; to always treat others (including customers, non-customers, shareholders, coworkers, vendors, and competitors) as they would expect to be treated. Although they are approved to represent Nordstrom, they must state that the views they express in their postings and other communications are their own. They are asked not to publish, post, or release information that is considered confidential or not meant for the public, such as strategies and forecasts; legal issues or future promotions and activities; merchandise pricing information or comparisons; nor should they give out private and personal information.

This being Nordstrom, their people are expected to be humble.

"Stay away from boasting about customer service," the company tells its employees involved in social networking. "As we all know, our number-one goal is to offer each customer great service but we're certainly not perfect and we do make mistakes. Let's stay focused on working to deliver great service instead of talking about it."

A personal stylist in Florida helps her customers do most of their shopping via e-mail and texts. "I can connect with them quickly and be more accessible. Before our Anniversary Sale, I edit down the choices appropriate for each customer, and then send small-resolution images that I get from Nordstrom.com or photos I take myself. Instead of spending 20 minutes on the phone trying to describe an item to a customer, it's right there in front of [him or her] on their computer or phone."

A women's wear salesperson in Seattle periodically takes pictures of items she thinks her customers would like and sends them via e-mail, text, Facebook, Twitter, and Tumblr.

"I always buy because she knows exactly what I have," wrote one of her customers. "She also knows what I need as a businesswoman and as a mom. Not just clothes, but also jewelry, shoes, cosmetics, and hosiery. I can tell her where I am going for a trip and what the weather is going to be. She sends me what I don't have and then e-mails a list of my outfits for the day. This is *a dream* for a busy person like me. Thank you for the social media platform. Without e-mail, Twitter, and Facebook, I would have to come in the store and I just don't have time. Ninety-nine percent of my purchases are handled through the mail. I would say that social media has also (at least) doubled my spending. Not in a frivolous way, but it exposes me to things that I just wouldn't have had time to look at for myself."

In an interview with *Loop*, the salesperson said that social media are "time-saving. I generate content from people, blogs, and news that I follow, so I can scroll and receive instant information all in one place. It makes the world much smaller, as I can follow people from all over the world."

Call Center Customer Service

You can't outsource customer service.

Few rewarding experiences come from talking to an outsourced call center. That's why Nordstrom doesn't farm out its customer service.

Instead, it gives the company a competitive edge, Jamie Nordstrom says, "where our folks are armed with all sorts of tools and information to take care of just about any issue a Nordstrom customer might have."

Nordstrom refers to its call center employees as "personal shoppers" because they are trained to help customers select the best fit and to suggest accessories and items that match the latest fashion trends. Much of Nordstrom's call center and order fulfillment services are based in Cedar Rapids, Iowa, where about 900 people are employed.

At Nordstrom, it's the job of everyone in the organization to ensure that every Nordstrom customer has access to the company and its merchandise whenever and wherever they want.

A customer and her daughter traveling from the East Coast to check out a college in Nebraska tried to use their GPS to locate the closest Nordstrom. They were directed to the Fulfillment Center in Cedar Rapids—there is no Nordstrom store in Iowa. When they walked into the center, they were confused and disappointed to find out it wasn't a store. The team at Cedar Rapids didn't miss a beat. They worked together to help the customers shop right there, using the website to find the items they wanted and then locating the merchandise on site. The pair drove away happy, excited, and in their words, "Nordstrom shoppers for life."

Answer the Telephone!

In many businesses, the telephone is a tool for exchanging voice mail messages, not for conducting an actual conversation. But even in the world of e-mail, texting, and websites, the telephone (as it was originally intended) is more important than ever.

How many times have you called a company and listened to a variation of the following message? "Thank you for calling ABC Company. Your call is important to us. Please note our menu has recently changed." Do you care if the menu has changed? Chances are, you didn't know what the previous menu was.

"Creating an inviting place" means devising a place—store, office, website—that best serves the customer. At Nordstrom stores, real people answer the phones during store hours; you never get an automated answering system telling you that your call is important. It's a subtle but distinctive reminder of Nordstrom service, which is available 24 hours a day, seven days a week. Specialists answer questions about customer accounts, upcoming events, store hours, locations, and whatever the customer needs to know.

The telephone is an essential tool for Van Mensah, a top menswear salesman in the Pentagon City store in suburban Washington, DC. His 3,000 active customers include many international business people and government officials.

"Some clients call me from their office, or overseas, or from their plane," says Mensah. "They'll say, 'I'm coming in from Europe and I need a suit and tie. I'm going to be in Washington for only a few hours and I have to fly to another location. Could you put this together for me?'"

Not surprisingly, whenever he's not selling to a customer in the store, Van is on the phone. He generally makes 25 to 30 customer calls per day. Many of the top performers at Nordstrom do the same thing, as well as sending out a similar number of e-mails and tweets.

The Nordstrom Family: Leading by Example

Within the company and the consuming public, the Nordstroms are approachable and accessible. All of them answer their own phones—and return calls. This has been true through four generations.

"I've taken thousands of calls over the years from customers who had one thing or another to say about how we were doing our business," Bruce Nordstrom wrote in his memoir, which included a story about Tom Peters, the noted author and speaker.

One day, while Bruce was sitting in his office, his phone rang. Bruce picked it up and said "Hello." After a second or two of silence, the voice on the other end asked, "Is this Bruce Nordstrom?"

Bruce said, "Yes."

After introducing himself, the man explained that he was on a break from a Tom Peters seminar in Toronto. Before the break, Peters had told his audience that the only executive he knew who answered his own phone was Bruce Nordstrom.

When the seminar went back in session after the break, Peters took the stage. Before he could get started, he saw a man in the audience waving his hand to be called on. It was the man who had called Bruce. He told everyone what he had just experienced. Big round of applause. Peters later sent Bruce a thank-you note for validating what he had said.

When Robert Spector told that story to a convention of dentists, one of the dentists came up later and said, "I don't usually answer the phone in my practice. If my staff is busy, I'll let the call go right to voice mail. But, you know, if Bruce Nordstrom isn't above answering his phone, I guess I'm not above it either."

Bruce's son Blake estimates that he gets 20 to 30 customer calls and 20 to 30 e-mails a day, plus letters.

Here's the story of one of those phone calls. Seattle resident Sarah Busch, then 79 years old, opened her monthly Nordstrom statement and was disappointed that the company had changed the format. She phoned Nordstrom's corporate headquarters and asked to speak to someone in management. After a few rings, a voice answered the phone.

"First of all, I'd like to know to whom I'm speaking," said Sarah Busch.

"This is Blake Nordstrom."

"Blake Nordstrom? You're the president!" a confounded Sarah Busch exclaimed.

"I am indeed."

"What are *you* doing answering the phone?"

"Well," Blake deadpanned, "I was sitting here at my desk, and the phone rang, so I picked it up."

She told Blake that she had been a loyal customer since Nordstrom was a shoe store and that she still had the first credit card Nordstrom issued when the company merged with Best Apparel in 1963 to become (temporarily) Nordstrom Best. She kept the card as a memento. But she didn't like the format of the new monthly statement.

Two days later, she received a letter from Blake, which included a brand-new replica of her old Nordstrom Best credit card. They've been friends ever since.

Next time your phone rings, please answer it. The party on the line could be one of your most loyal customers.

10

The Sale Is Never Over

Establish, Nurture, and Sustain Long-Term Relationships With Your Customers

When our customers have a "go-to" salesperson who's in tune with their style and budget, they spend more. Customers appreciate having one person they can count on for all their wardrobe needs, because it saves them time and they leave our store happier with their purchases. And happy customers become repeat customers.

—The Nordstrom employee newsletter, *Loop*

Asked about the best advice he gives his shoe salespeople, Bruce Nordstrom replied: "I tell them to measure both feet."

Measure both feet? In the literal sense, a knowledgeable shoe salesperson will measure both feet because she knows that a customer's right foot might be a slightly different size than the left foot. So, by measuring both feet, she is showing the customer that she's a professional, that she knows what she's doing. Nordstrom people are trained to understand the nature and anatomy of the foot, in order to insure the best fit.

As we have previously mentioned, if a customer has more than a size-and-a-half difference between his or her right and left feet, Nordstrom splits sizes so that the customer doesn't have to buy two full pair of shoes.

Just as important as the actual measurement is the salesperson's taking the time to talk to the customer and to begin planting the seeds of a relationship by asking pertinent questions. What kind of business are you in? Are you on your feet all day? Do you need dress shoes or more casual shoes? Do you play sports? Do you need shoes for those activities? Do you have foot problems? All the while, that salesperson is creating a relationship by taking note of what the customer is telling him or her. The salesperson is using his product knowledge and awareness of trends to make a connection with the customer and to sell more merchandise.

The key is making a connection.

After purchasing a prom dress for her 16-year-old daughter, a mother went to the shoe department to find matching shoes for the dress. She mentioned to a Nordstrom saleswoman that her daughter walks with crutches and wears braces on her feet that go halfway up her shin. She always had to wear "ugly, clunky" shoes to formal affairs. The saleswoman encouraged the mother to come back to the store with her daughter and she would help to find the perfect shoe. A few days later, when mother and daughter returned, the Nordstrom saleswoman brought out a shoe that matched perfectly. The teenager "tried it on her like she was Cinderella," wrote the mother in a letter to Nordstrom management. "It fit!!!!!!"

The daughter, mother, and saleswoman discussed whether to have a shoemaker add a bit of "insurance" (a strap or tie) to make sure the shoe would stay on. The saleswoman suggested that if they added a strap, they could hide it with a bow. As the mother and daughter were leaving, the saleswoman asked them to return with a picture of the girl at the prom, which they did.

Customer Loyalty

Until he retired in 2000 after almost three decades, Patrick McCarthy was the quintessential Nordstrom employee. For the last 25 of those years, McCarthy sold men's tailored clothing in the downtown Seattle flagship store, and was number one in sales throughout the chain for an astonishing 15 years in a row.

An entrepreneurial self-starter like all top Nordstrom salespeople, McCarthy, who considered himself "a franchise within a franchise," was, in his day, one of the best-known salesmen in Seattle. He drew from a personal client list of 7,000 people, ranging from recent college graduates to chief executive officers and United States senators.

McCarthy tells the story of playing golf one day with a couple of people who didn't know who he was. At the first tee, one stranger who was in his foursome asked the typical question: "What do you do for a living?"

To which McCarthy replied: "I sell a relationship."

The questioner flashed a quizzical look, and then returned to the golf game. But at the second hole, he had to ask the question again: "No, really, what do you do for a living?"

McCarthy replied: "I sell men's suits at Nordstrom."

"Oh, so that's what you do," said the stranger, fully satisfied with the answer.

"No," McCarthy replied. "That's not what I do. What I do is sell relationships."

And that's exactly what all successful businesses and salespeople do—sell relationships.

It is axiomatic that people like to do business with people they like. If your product or service is similar to your competitor's, and the price for that product or service is similar to that of your competitor, what will be the reason why you will get the business and not your competitor? The answer to that question is the relationship you have with your customer and the trust you have built up over time. Once you've established and nurtured that relationship, and you've continued to work at the relationship (and never take it for granted), why should your customer go anywhere else?

Nordstrom is constantly reinforcing the value of relationships to its sales force because a loyal customer invariably goes back to the same salesperson. That's how you build your business—by being trustworthy, reliable, keeping your promises, and making adjustments along the way as conditions change.

"A lot of times, salespeople are in a rush to make a quick sale," said Van Mensah, a top men's clothing salesman at the Fashion Centre at Pentagon City, Virginia. "But a quick sale is not nearly as valuable as a long-term relationship. If a customer is looking for a specific item, you do everything possible to find it for him. Do a merchandise search and DTC [Direct to Customer] shipment to his house. Check our online store. Or call a buyer or the vendor. I don't think I'm providing the customer with good service unless I exhaust all the avenues within the company to satisfy the customer's needs. That extra effort is going to sustain your business in the long run."

McCarthy's first indication of the value of selling a relationship came when he joined Nordstrom in 1971 and saw how Ray Black, then the company's most successful men's clothing salesman, made a living from the relationships he had developed. Black remembered customers' names and previous purchases. He was so good that customers would come into the Nordstrom menswear department and ask for him. If he wasn't working that day, they would leave and come back on a day when he would be there.

A women's sportswear department manager in a Nordstrom store in California said that the best way to connect with customers is to be yourself.

"When I first started with Nordstrom I would look at different salespeople and think, 'Wow, I would sure like to sell like that!' Or 'Why do her customers always greet her with a big hug and offer to buy her coffee?'

"I've learned that you establish those types of relationships by being genuine, asking friendly questions, and really listening to the customer. Once you earn the customer's trust, you can bring out your personality and guide her to all kinds of things she wants and needs. I might say, 'Let's go for a walk. Let me show you something I just saw down in Women's Active.' I'm just being myself. It's like we're two friends going shopping together."

Customer loyalty is the coin of the realm in business. Nordstrom salespeople generate that loyalty by taking ownership of the customer and the customer experience. But what's even more remarkable about the Nordstrom culture is how customers feel about Nordstrom salespeople. When Robert Spector speaks to business groups, invariably someone in the audience will come up after his presentation and start the conversation by saying, "I have this Nordstrom salesman," and proceed to tell a story about outstanding customer service—either one spectacular example or just a description of a good, solid, steady relationship that has grown over the course of several years.

In most sales cultures, salespeople are always claiming a customer as their own. But when a customer claims a salesperson as his or her own, that's powerful; that's a relationship.

Do you know what can make a difference in the relationship? Remembering the customer's name. Customers want and expect to be recognized by the people they shop with. According to Nordstrom, of all the questions the company asks its customers, the one that most highly connects with how much money they spend is: "Does the salesperson remember me from my last visit?" When you remember customers' names, it gives the customers the feeling that they are important and that their business is valued.

A longtime Pacesetter in men's sportswear in the Northeast said, "I like to address the customer by name—and repeat my name often, so they start to know who I am. You start with the introduction, then you put them in your personal book and you send a thank-you note. Then you call to follow up with their purchase or alterations. Each time they hear your name, it adds familiarity."

A top seller in a women's department in California remarked, "As simple as it sounds, it's very important to look the customer in the eye and call her by name. Then you need to learn her style and her size. When she comes back, you can pull her size right away and say, 'These jeans should fit you perfectly.'"

That kind of relationship engenders loyalty.

"Loyalty is why I fly in [to Phoenix] from Santa Fe, New Mexico, twice a month to get products," wrote a customer about a salesperson named Thomas. "Loyalty is never hesitating on where I'm going to shop for a new pair of shoes, or a Michele watch for my better half, or even those custom shirts that you all make for me that fit so perfectly. Loyalty, in a world of many options, does not come easy and is very hard to learn. I commend Thomas for solidifying my loyalty to Nordstrom."

One successful saleswoman uses e-mail to keep in touch with busy customers, one of whom was a high-level assistant to the president of her firm, who often traveled to Europe. "I would study her travel plans via e-mail, so I could schedule her alterations appointments, or find a dress for a special event or a new suit if she was meeting with a foreign dignitary," said the saleswoman.

A Customer Service All-Star and Personal Stylist in a store in the southeastern United States believes getting to know the customer on a personal level leads to more repeat visits. "I try to find out everything I can about my customers and get to know their family, too," he said. "If a man doesn't like to shop, I try to get him in the fitting room with a few things, offer him a cup of coffee, then keep bringing him stuff to try on. Meanwhile, I'm asking questions, 'Do you wear a tie to work? Do you have kids? What kind of hobbies do you have?' When the customer leaves, I make notes in my personal book. That way, when I follow up or they come back in, they feel like they're dealing with a friend."

A Pacesetter and Customer Service All-Star in men's sportswear noted that opportunities abound "when you see each customer as a real person. It's important to spend a little extra time with the customer, just to learn little things like their hobbies, where they grew up, or where their kids play volleyball. Those little details help make your follow-up calls and cards more friendly and personal."

Personal Stylist

Nordstrom wants to grow more of those loyal, personal relationships because they drive sales and improve the shopping experience.

Although today's customers shop via more than one channel, Nordstrom found in a survey that three-quarters of its customers still desire a relationship with at least one top-performing salesperson they know and trust. To that end, the company initiated a program called "Get Connected" that matched almost 60,000 high-spend customers with a "personal stylist"—a go-to salesperson who can take care of all his or her needs. The customer is not charged extra for shopping with the personal stylist. The program has produced tens of millions of dollars in additional sales.

Stylists, who generally work by appointment, are empowered to sell the clients any merchandise in any department throughout the store. Consequently, they are generally better versed than most of the other store employees in what the whole store has to offer. As the relationship develops, the stylist gets a more intimate look at the client's wardrobe, lifestyle, and current needs.

A business owner from Chicago, who shopped exclusively online, was connected with a stylist at the Michigan Avenue store by a Nordstrom customer relationship manager. The customer described her first encounter with the stylist as "a luxury experience. Now I don't really shop with anyone else."

A fashion blogger wrote about her Nordstrom personal stylist: "I've never felt pressured by Kelly to buy anything. In fact, she's stepped in a few times, and told me not to buy something because: (a) I didn't need it; (b) I had something similar already; (c) it was a super trendy piece I probably wouldn't get a lot of wear out of. She's my insider at the store, so if I ever need help with a return or finding an item, I just need to shoot her an e-mail or send her a text."

A customer wrote a letter to Nordstrom about her salesperson in the Seattle area, who did "all my shopping and acted as my personal shopper, even outside the department. I run a very large company, travel a lot, have three children, and need to look good, which means I frequently need to mix and match when traveling. Our relationship spans about seven years, and I truly don't know what I would do without her or without the social media she employs. On average, I buy 50 percent of any key pieces she puts on Twitter. Her Facebook pages (especially the designer page she just started) are a reminder for me to check online and see what has come in that I might like."

Listen to the Customer/Stay in Touch

For successful salespeople, the process of customer service starts by just listening to the customer, determining his or her needs, and providing solutions through the resources and merchandise at his or her disposal.

Those encounters may begin with a simple, friendly greeting. From there, it helps to be curious and inquisitive about what brought the customer into the store and all the activities going on in his or her life.

The best service providers ask good questions and are good listeners. Then, in a genuine and positive way, they try to see things through the customers' eyes and come up with solutions.

A Pacesetter on the East Coast sees selling as the outcome of her primary focus, which is communicating. "I don't think you can be successful at Nordstrom unless you have a reason to communicate with the customer other than, 'I have something to sell you.' I like to spend a lot of time in the fitting room, asking questions, learning about the customer's life, and sharing stories. Of course, I also keep them up to date on what's happening in the store and what items they might be interested in."

A longtime Pacesetter in women's wear in California keeps in touch with customers through e-mail, alerting them to post-holiday markdowns and new arrivals. "I don't come right out and say, 'Can I have your e-mail address?' I cultivate the relationship first with a written thank-you and a follow-up phone call. Then I'll ask, 'Do you have an e-mail address? I'd love to communicate that way, if it's easier for you.' Most of my customers find it very convenient."

A successful Nordstrom shoe salesman has a special way of following up with customers who recently bought a pair of shoes from him. A couple of days after the purchase, he calls the customer and asks how the shoes are working out. "Ninety percent of the time, they're so stunned that you called that they remember you," said the salesman, who then invites the customer back to get his shoes shined (with the salesman picking up the tab). That offer gets the customer back into the store, where the salesman has the opportunity to sell him another pair of shoes—or at least to stop by and stay hello.

The Personal Book

Personal books have been a part of the arsenal for Nordstrom salespeople for many years. In the old days, personal books were loose-leaf notebooks that contained vital information on every customer, including phone numbers, credit card numbers, names of spouse and children, previous purchases, sizes, vendor preferences, likes and dislikes, special orders, and any other characteristics, such as being a difficult fit or preferring to shop during sales events, and so on.

Today, personal books are no longer physical notebooks; they are all computerized in a customer-service software package. Salespeople can easily access their own customer base, create lists, and follow up with customers more efficiently.

The more information a salesperson can remember about his or her customers, the easier it is for them to shop. By remembering pertinent information about their customers, salespeople become more closely connected with those customers.

According to an internal Nordstrom survey, the company's top sellers (more than $1 million in sales) said that 68 percent of their business comes from personal trade, which makes the personal book an invaluable tool.

A saleswoman in women's shoes in the Pacific Northwest knows customers may not be able to afford everything they want each time they visit. "I write down the item the customer really wanted but didn't have time to buy or couldn't afford on the back of my business card. I'll also enter that information in my personal book. Often, those people will come back in and say, 'Hey, I'm ready to get those boots now!' You need to develop a rapport first, so the customer has fun shopping with you, wherever you decide to go."

Nordstrom Weddings

What better way to establish a potentially long-term relationship than to help with a customer's wedding plans? Most department stores have conceded the bridal salon business to specialty stores and independent retailers over the past two decades. They had a hard time justifying the salon when more profitable departments were waiting for floor space.

But Nordstrom sees growth in this area. Although the company had been assisting customers with their wedding attire and accessories for years, it dramatically expanded its efforts with wedding shops in several of its stores. Personal stylists are trained to help outfit and accessorize the entire wedding party with reception dresses, bridesmaid dresses, shoes, headpieces, jewelry, and foundations. Apple iPads are provided so brides can search the web to show the stylists what kinds of gowns they like (and so friends and family waiting for the bride to try on her gown can entertain themselves). The social networking elements on nordstrom.com enable brides to share their thoughts and ideas with friends and other brides-to-be. There is also a dedicated Nordstrom Weddings page on Facebook.

Relationships With Vendors

At Nordstrom, the importance of relationships extends to its vendors, who play an active role in the business all the way to the selling floor. Nordstrom wants its vendors to have relationships with salespeople and department managers to help with presentation and product knowledge. Nordstrom holds its vendors accountable. Product is everything. Loyalty is required; it's not optional.

Nordstrom is well known for taking a chance on a vendor, nurturing that relationship, and helping that vendor grow—not only within Nordstrom, but also within the retail industry. One example is the shoe company named for its founder, Steve Madden, who told *Women's Wear Daily*, "Clearly there would not be a Steve Madden brand without Nordstrom. . . . They allowed entrepreneurs like myself to have a national base."

Brands covet an invitation to win shelf space. Madden recalls the first time he was asked to attend a Nordstrom buyer's meeting. "It was like an invite to the White House."

Ever since 1992, the company has awarded its Nordstrom Partners in Excellence Award to vendors "whose products and business practices best exemplify our commitments to quality and value, service, partnership, business ethics, fashion, and results."

Nordstrom wanted to find a way "to recognize the people who do it the best; people who not only make the best products but are honest and ethical and really a pleasure to be partners with; people who care about our success and people whose success we care about," said Bruce Nordstrom.

Past winners include the Estée Lauder Companies, Tommy Bahama, Josie Natori, the Hickey-Freeman Company, UGGs shoes, Juicy Couture, Hugo Boss, and the Dexter Shoe Company.

As it moves into its twelfth decade of business, Nordstrom's values have remained unchanged. A strategy built around customer service continues to be what separates this company from its retail competitors. Although the ways in which it takes care of customers must adapt with the times and the technology, the company is constant and steadfast in its belief that the customer remains the best filter for every business decision it makes, both large and small.

The first edition of this book, published in 1995, concluded with a quote from cochairman emeritus John N. Nordstrom, of the third generation of the family, and grandson of founder John W. Nordstrom. It remains just as relevant today.

"Our commitment is 100 percent to customer service. If I'm a salesperson on the floor and I know that the people that run this place are committed to customer service, then I am free to find new ways to give great customer service. I know I won't be criticized for taking care of a customer. I will only be criticized if I don't take care of a customer."

PHASE III

APPLICATIONS

How to Become the Nordstrom of Your Industry

Now that you see how the Nordstrom Way works, how can you translate Nordstrom's methods to your organization? In this final phase of the book, you will learn how to use these applications to the preceding chapters in order to evaluate your current customer service efforts and create a road map that will improve your customer service approach throughout your entire organization.

In order for these exercises to work for the long haul, the leadership of your organization must be intimately involved every step of the way and must set a shining example. Everyone needs to know that it takes hard work and constant vigilance to maintain the highest level of customer service.

Following are the applications that pertain to the material discussed in the preceding 10 chapters. By far the greatest number of Applications are related to Chapter 3, which covers mentoring, supporting, praise, recognition, and reward, because these are the essential elements for a culture of customer service.

Chapter 1: Tell the Story ────────────────────────

Application 1: What Is Our Company's History?

Most companies and organizations have an interesting history. After all, they were created for specific reasons, such as filling a void in the market, coming up with a new idea, introducing a new product, and so on. Appoint one of your employees to be the unofficial company historian. That person will assemble relevant documents, news articles, and corporate reports, and interview founders or other key executives to get a flavor of the company's history and, ultimately, its culture.

Answer the following questions:

- Who founded the company?
- Why was the company founded?
- What kind of challenges did the founder face?
- Was there a time when it looked like the company was headed for failure?
- How was the company able to overcome adversity and survive?
- How has the company changed its business over the years?
- How has the company responded and adapted to changes in the market?

Once the information is assembled, distribute it to all members of your organization. Make it fun. Assign a committee of employees to come up with a *Jeopardy*-like program that covers your company history. Organize a group of employees who have studied the material. Encourage them to play the *Jeopardy* game. This can be fun and educational. Don't forget to include prizes.

Application 2: What Do We Stand for?

Brainstorm the qualities that make your organization and your culture unique. Compile a list of these qualities and disseminate the list throughout your organization. We are not asking you to create a mission statement. Mission statements are generally the products of committees, and they sound that way. Nordstrom has no mission statement.

Assemble a group of people from all parts of your organization.

Give everyone a pad and pen. Give them 10 minutes to answer these questions:

1. What do we stand for?
2. What are the qualities that make our organization unique?
3. How do we see ourselves?
4. How do our competitors see us?
5. How do our customers see us?
6. How do our suppliers see us?

Put together a master list of all your answers and then:

- Discuss the results.
- Edit the results down to a few workable sentences that encapsulate what the company stands for.
- Post these results all over the company through e-mail, printed posters, on presentation decks, and so on. These words should be a living part of your culture.
- Include the list in your employee handbook.
- Encourage and reward employees who live up to those qualities.

Application 3: Tell the Story of Your Company's Heroes

As we have seen, storytelling is an essential way for Nordstrom to promote and sustain its culture. There are great stories in your organization. Your assignment is to find them and spread the word about them. These stories should include both internal and external customers.

- Ask employees to submit great stories of customer service.
- Ask employees to submit great stories of teamwork among employees.
- Offer prizes for the best stories.
- Find ways to encourage, honor, and reward outstanding acts of customer service.

Chapter 2: Hire With Care: Finding the Right Fit for the Culture

Application 1: Finding Great Talent

Be proactive in your search for great talent to join your organization.

- Select an employee to represent your company's recruiting efforts.
- Encourage employees to hand out business cards to great employment candidates.
- Train them to always be on the lookout for talent—while at dinner, shopping, traveling, anywhere!
- Participate in social networking.
- Participate in your community networking.
- Attend college campus recruiting days and community job fairs.

Application 2: Hiring Questionnaire

How do you find people who are service- and results-oriented and who are also team players? First of all, when you are interviewing them, you must ask them the right questions.

- Assemble a broad cross section of your longtime employees in one room or via a conference call or virtual meeting.
- Select a person to lead the discussion.
- Compile a list of qualities that elicit the following attributes in new hires.
    1. A sense of customer service.
    2. A definition of customer service.
    3. A desire to give customer service.
    4. A willingness to work hard.
    5. Self–motivation.
    6. Independence.
    7. Judgment.
    8. Creativity.
    9. Dealing with difficult customers.
    10. Teamwork.
    11. An ability to achieve results.
    12. A competitive spirit.
- Distribute this list to the rest of your company.
- Organize the list and make it a formal element for selecting new hires.

Application 3: Internship Programs

Part of developing the best talent in your organization includes welcoming future talent. If your company is of sufficient size to support it, create an internship program.

- Identify areas in need of support and innovation, which also provide opportunity for career advancement and/or that teach and apply applicable skills.
- Create criteria for the hiring process.
- If your company or organization is the place to do so, select an employee to head the internship program. Otherwise, create a team of people to drive the initiative.
- Design a curriculum for the program that spells out specific projects and goals.
- Visit college career fairs and work with college career offices to find intern candidates and to promote your internship program.

Chapter 3: Nurture the Nordie: Mentor Support, Praise, Recognize, and Reward

Application 1: New Hire Orientation

Devise a varied and interactive experience for your new hires.

- Create a culture trivia game.
- Conduct discussions between tenured employees and new hires about your company's customer experience.
- Create presentations that explain what sets your organization apart from your competition.
- Bring in guest speakers, such as top-performing employees and upper management.
- Get the new hires excited before they begin their jobs.

Application 2: Create a Meaningful Experience for Your Employees

How does your company inspire employees to feel that their work has greater meaning than just being a job?

- Delegate responsibility to your employees.
- Empower employees to solve their own problems, which enables them to be heroes to their customers.
- Motivate employees with inspirational signage and empower them with accessible bulletin boards to share ideas and celebrate achievement.
- Create a list of meaningful and inspiring quotations.
- Post them throughout your organization.
- Open the bulletin boards for inspirational photos, exciting new initiatives, and customer feedback. This is a place for your employees to show their pride in the company that they work for.

Application 3: Make Your Company Special

- Create a contest similar to Nordstrom's Make Nordstrom Special, where employees are encouraged to come up with promotions and suggestions to drive results.
- Create a meaningful reward for the winners.
- Make this contest a regular part of your culture.

Application 4: Praise Your Employees

- Ask each employee to recommend a fellow employee who gives great customer service.
- Write a note of recognition and praise for that person.
- Send the note to that person.

Application 5: Develop Talent; Create a Promote-From-Within Philosophy

Inspire your current talent to climb the ladder of success by offering them a promote-from-within program. Again, when employees are offered opportunity for growth, they are more loyal to your company and products and more inspired to contribute to your company experience.

This program could include opportunities for relocation, department transfers, and management training.

Application 6: Professional Development Programs

How does your company help employees discover and develop their talents, challenge themselves professionally, manage their careers, and/or enhance their personal growth?

Offer continuing education in the following areas:

- Conflict resolution
- Project management
- Basic writing workshops
- Self-development
- Presentation skills
- Time management
- Effective people skills

Application 7: For the New Hire: Get to Know Your Coworkers

Encourage new hires to meet with as many other team members as possible.

- Create a get-to-know-you game for these new hires.
- Reward these new hires for their knowledge of new coworkers. Award them bonus points for the more details they can remember, such as job titles, length of service, and so on.

Application 8: Celebrations and Holidays

Celebrate birthdays, holidays, and other special occasions for your employees and customers.

- Announce employee birthdays and personal achievements, such as births, weddings, hobby accomplishments, and so on.
- Keep track of customer birthdays and send a card. Offer a discount or small gift valid during their birthday week.

Application 9: Organize Monthly Recognition Meetings

- Select a committee to create and organize the meetings.
- Empower the committee to organize an agenda.
- Decide on a purpose and objective for the meeting.
- Create awards and other forms of recognition.
- Have the meeting.
- Record the meeting so that the committee can critique it later.
- Distribute feedback forms to those in attendance. Get their comments on the meeting, and incorporate those suggestions into the planning for the next meeting.

Application 10: Empathy

Train your employees to understand empathy and the impact it has on people buying from them. This includes conversation and strategy based on thinking and feeling, hearing, saying and doing, and seeing pain plus gain. The priority is for your team of employees to understand the difference between themselves and their customers, which is critical to increased sales.

Example: Instead of the traditional question, "What can we sell customers?" ask this question: "What can we do to improve our customers' experience?"

Application 11: How Do We Develop Our Employees?

Gather a cross section of your employees, both managers and front-line people. Discuss whether you have a culture that encourages and mentors new and long-standing employees. Ask these questions:

- How do we manage our employees?
- How do we mentor those employees?
- How do we retain our great employees?
- How can we establish an internal mentor program (whether formal or informal)?
- How do we set a positive customer service example for our employees and managers?
- Do we pat people on the back?
- Do we tell people they are appreciated?
- If the answers to those last two questions are "no," then how do we find a way to turn those answers into "yes"?

Application 12: Wellness Programs

How does your company help employees balance their work with personal or family lives? To ensure that employees are creating the best customer experience, ask yourselves if you are creating the best employee experience. Employees who are supported outside of the workplace will give superior service during work.

Offer:

- Onsite health screenings
- Health portals
- Exercise trackers
- Meal planners
- Health coaching
- Informational articles
- Health classes
- Flu shots
- Work-from-home programs
- Emergency readiness

Application 13: Goal Setting

- Assemble several people from all departments of your company.
- Direct those people to brainstorm on company goals, both individual and collective. Make sure goals are easily measurable and when achieved are visible to your organization.
- Compile an official list of those goals and distribute them to everyone in the organization.
- Set target dates for reaching goals. Set a time line of ambitious but reachable steps.

Chapter 4: Empower Entrepreneurs to Own the Customer Experience

Application 1: What Does Empowerment Mean?

- Define the word "empowerment" and write down that definition.
- Compare your definition with those of the other people in the group.

- Ask yourself if "empowerment," as defined, exists in your organization.
- If so, write down all the ways that empowerment is illustrated in your organization.
- Once you have compiled that list, review each of those illustrations of empowerment and discuss how each has benefited your organization.
- How can the value of empowerment become a core value of your company?
- How can you encourage employees to feel they are empowered?

Application 2: For the Individual Employee: Create Your Own System

Assuming that you are empowered by your employers to do whatever it takes to take care of the customer, how do you create your own system within the larger system?

- List the duties and requirements of your job.
- List the choices that your employer has given you to best take care of the customer.
- List the choices you have that will best fit you, your personality, and how you like to do business.
- List the reasons for those options and how they can work for both you and your organization

Application 3: Examine and Break Your Rules

- Bring out your rule books, employee manuals, and procedure lists.
- Assign a group of people to review all these materials.

- Ask them to write all the rules, procedures, and so forth that are internal. (We are not talking about rules over which you have no control, such as mandated legislation or regulation.)
- Have people in your organization vote on those lists: What rules belong? What rules need to be eliminated?
- Eliminate all the rules that come between you and your customer.

Chapter 5: Compensate According to Results

Application 1: Models of Motivational Compensation

- List all of the ways that compensation and bonuses have an impact on empowerment in your organization.
- Discuss creative ways to use compensation to improve empowerment and entrepreneurship among employees.

Chapter 6: Communication and Teamwork: We're All in the Customer Service Department

Application 1: Teamwork Requirements

Nordstrom has a list of requirements to promote team goals.

- Assemble a group of people from all departments within your organization. Their assignment is to do the following things:
  - Create your own list of requirements for team goals.
  - Distribute those requirements for team goals.
  - Ensure that those requirements become an essential part of your culture.

Application 2: Team Achievement

Do you honor team achievement within your organization? Make team achievement part of your culture.

- Assemble a group of people from all departments within your organization. Their assignment is to do the following things:
  - Create categories for team achievement.
  - Devise awards for honoring team achievement.
  - Determine the criteria for winning each award.
  - Determine how frequently you will award team achievement.
  - Determine how each award will be judged.

Application 3: How Can I Make Your Life Easier?

Look beyond yourself. Focus instead on the customer or fellow employee standing in front of you. Ask yourself: "What can I do to make his or her life easier?"

- Each day, have your organization focus on three colleagues and/or three customers.
- Intentionally make a positive effort to make their lives easier.
- Celebrate the people who are making an impact on others.

Habit creates routine, routine creates excellence. Before you know it, your company or organization will be looking to make everyone else's life a little easier.

Application 4: Team Building

Look at each of your company's departments. Ask each of them to test their infrastructure through team building exercises.

For example: On one morning each quarter, members of Nordstrom's maintenance team compete against each other to see who can run up and down the store's escalators the fastest. This lighthearted race builds unity through friendly competition and a break from hard work. What exercises can you create at your workplace to emphasize the importance of teamwork in your culture?

Application 5: Internal Communications

Internal communications should be used to keep employees informed, to congratulate successes, and to inspire growth. Employees who are kept in the know on company happenings are empowered employees.

- Start an internal newsletter that highlights company and personal achievements.
- Prominently display bulletin boards that keep employees updated on sales results, departmental activities, and company-wide notices.
- Send regular e-mail updates.

Chapter 7: Citizen Nordstrom: Doing Well, Doing Good

Application 1: Going Green

As part of your corporate social responsibility, does your company have a "green team"? Being green is much more than using brown paper bags instead of plastic. If you are interested in putting together a green team, select a green leader within your company or organization. Consider these ideas:

- Designate a green leader in each of your departments.
- Take a company-wide assessment to identify potential impact or improvement areas.

- Share what you find and spread the ideas company-wide. Post them so that the entire company is in the loop.
- Encourage people to be positive contributors.
- Keep updates in the company loop.
- Lead by example, no matter what your role in the company.

Application 2: How Do You Give Back to the Community?

Think about the impact your company has on your community. First, define your community: Whom does your organization affect?

- Support the communities in which you do business. Learn how you can help with any issues the community is facing.
- Learn where your products come from. Work to protect human rights and evaluate your impact on that community.
- Sustain the environment for all communities of which your company is a part.
- Develop incentive programs for employees who volunteer their time outside of work. Schedule service outings for your organization.
- Leave your company better than you found it.

Chapter 8: Create an Inviting Place: Brick-and-Mortar Still Matters

Application 1: Think Like the Customer

Is your place of business an inviting place? Do your customers feel that they are important? It's easy to find the answers to those questions.

- Select several people in your organization and give them this assignment.

- Walk into your place of business as if you've never been there. Pretend you are the customer. Write down the following:
  - What do you see?
  - What don't you see?
  - Is everything clearly marked?
  - Is there someone there to help you?
  - What do you like?
  - What don't you like?
  - What would you like to change?
- After everyone has completed this assignment, reconvene the group and compare your answers. Clearly, if everyone is finding similar problems, it is time to address those problems.
- Assign some of the people in the group to institute changes that make your business a customer-friendly place.

Application 2: Call Your Company, Surf Your Website, and Interact With Your Company and Customers through Social Media

As in the previous exercise, pretend you are the customer.

- Call your company, as if you were a customer.
- Ask to speak to a particular person whom you know is out of the office.
- Ask a question about a product or service.
- Gather people who work in all aspects of your business to evaluate the efficiency and customer-friendly qualities of your website. List all of the places where people are likeliest to abandon your site.
- Are your social media updated regularly? Are they useful? Do they add to the customer experience?
- Make notes on what works and what doesn't.

- Again, as in the previous exercise, reconvene your team to compare notes, and then find ways to improve all aspects of your customer experience.

Chapter 9: Touchpoints: Multichannel Customer Service

Application 1: Getting Feedback From the Customer

The more information you get from your customer the better able you are to take care of your customer.

- Make a list of the communication choices your organization offers your customers.
- How does your customer like to communicate with your company?
- Make a list of all the questions you can ask your customer in order to better understand your customer's communication needs.
- Compare and combine your list with those of your colleagues. Then come up with a master list of the best series of questions to promote the best in customer service.

Application 2: Ask the Question: What Does Great Customer Service Mean to You?

What's the formula for giving great customer service? The answer depends on the individual being served. Some customers are in a hurry; others prefer a more leisurely experience. To gain perspective on what customer service means to your customers, ask them. The more information you have the better able you are to take care of your customer.

- Select a company or organization leader to identify your top customers and do the following things.
- Make a list of the choices your organization offers your customers.

- Make a list of all the questions you can ask your customer in order to better understand your customers' needs.
- Compare and combine your list with those of your colleagues. Then come up with a master list of the best series of questions to promote the best in customer service.
- Identify your top customers with varying profiles.
- Ask them this question: "What does customer service mean to you?"
- Use this information to streamline your customer service practices.

Chapter 10: The Sale Is Never Over: Establish, Nurture, and Sustain Long-Term Relationships with Your Customers _____

Application 1: Tracking Spheres of Influence

How did you get that client?

- Make a list of your longest standing customers.
- Ask them what's keeping them with your company.
- Devise ways to reward those clients for their loyalty.
- Follow through by rewarding them for their loyalty.

Application 2: How Do Your Customers Experience Your Product?

- How do your customers hear about your company or organization's products or services?
- When your customers are using your product or service, how would you and your customers evaluate the user experience?
- What happens after your customers are through using your products or services?

Application 3: Vendor as Partners

If you expect excellence from your employees, you should expect the same from your partners and vendors.

- Compile a list of qualities that elicit the following attributes in vendors and suppliers.
    1. A sense of customer service.
    2. A definition of customer service.
    3. A desire to give customer service.
    4. A willingness to work hard.
    5. Judgment.
    6. Creativity.
    7. Dealing with difficult situations.
    8. A competitive spirit.
- Make a list of your best vendors and suppliers.
- Devise ways to reward them for their loyalty.
- Emulating Nordstrom's "Partners in Excellence," create an official program to reward your vendors and suppliers.

Application 3: Cultivate a Relationship

How do you develop a relationship with your customers?

- Gather a cross section of your colleagues for a brainstorming session on how each one of you develops the relationship.
- Prepare a list of questions that you ask your customers.
- Distribute this list to everyone in your organization.
- Ask them to add to this list.
- Make this list of questions a standard feature in your training.
- If your phone rings, answer it.
- If you get an e-mail, reply to it.

Acknowledgments

My Nordstrom journey began in 1982, when I became a regular freelance correspondent in Seattle for *Women's Wear Daily* and the other trade newspapers that then comprised Fairchild Publications.

One of the first companies I wrote about was Nordstrom, which was then a strictly West Coast retail chain, but was beginning to gain a national reputation for its culture of customer service. As a native of New Jersey, whose first job out of college was writing retail advertising for a division of Macy's, I was fascinated by the Nordstrom culture of taking care of the customer. I remain fascinated to this day.

In 1990, I was contacted by Elizabeth Wales, a Seattle literary agent, whose next-door neighbor was Patrick D. McCarthy, then Nordstrom's number-one salesman. They had an idea for a book on McCarthy and Nordstrom, and asked me if I was interested in writing it. You know what my answer was.

Five years later, in 1995, the hardcover, *The Nordstrom Way: The Inside Story of America's Number One Customer Service Company*, was published by John Wiley & Sons. It quickly became a business best seller. Since then, there has been a second edition hardcover, a quality trade paperback, a mass-market paperback, and a handbook, *The Nordstrom Way to Customer Service Excellence: A Handbook for Implementing Great Service in Your Organization*, which combined elements of the original *The Nordstrom Way* and my 2001 book, *Lessons from the Nordstrom Way: How Companies Are Emulating the #1 Customer Service Company*, which profiled the customer service efforts of a variety of firms (big and small) in other industries.

This book is more than a second edition of *The Nordstrom Way to Customer Service Excellence*. It is a brand-new book, which represents a reexamining of three decades of my researching, observing, experiencing, and talking to corporate audiences all over the world about this endlessly intriguing company. I've had the opportunity to interview—and tell the stories of—three generations of Nordstroms, as well as countless executives, managers, buyers, and front-line salespeople, most notably Patrick McCarthy.

The names on an author's acknowledgments page cannot accurately reflect the vast number of people who helped to make *The Nordstrom Way*, in all its versions, possible.

Deep and heartfelt thanks to:

Pat McCarthy for his belief in the Nordstrom way and for his shining example for generations of Nordstrom employees.

The cochairmen of the third generation of company leadership—Bruce, John N., and the late Jim Nordstrom, and Jack McMillan—for their cooperation and trust in the original book, and for the use of three privately published family memoirs: *The Immigrant,* published in 1887 by founder John W. Nordstrom; *A Winning Team: The Story of Everett, Elmer & Lloyd Nordstrom,* by Elmer Nordstrom; and *Leave It Better Than You Found It,* by Bruce Nordstrom.

The leaders of the fourth generation of Nordstroms—Blake, Peter, and Erik—for sharing their insights.

Brooke White, corporate public relations director, for her invaluable help.

Richard Narramore, my editor at John Wiley & Sons, for shepherding this project with the highest professionalism and for giving me the rare opportunity to revisit, reshape, revise, and expand this material. And to Lydia Dimitriadis and Deborah Schindlar for their careful editing.

BreAnne O. Reeves, chief executive officer of Robert Spector Consulting, for her invaluable assistance in helping me create the Applications section of this book.

Elizabeth Wales, the best agent (and stalwart friend) an author could ask for.

Marybeth Spector, who sustains me every day in every way and is the ideal spouse for an author—at least this one.

ROBERT SPECTOR
Seattle, Washington

Index